SAMURAI FIGHTING ARTS

SAMURAI FIGHTING ARTS

The Spirit and the Practice

FUMON TANAKA

KODANSHA INTERNATIONAL
Tokyo • New York • London

The names of modern and contemporary Japanese appear in the Western order, while those of historical figures (pre–1868) are written in the traditional order; surname preceding given name.

For reference, the following chart shows those periods of Japanese history which will be most relevant to the discussion.

PERIOD NAME	APPROXIMATE DATES (A.D.)
Nara	710–84
Heian	794–1192
Kamakura	1192–1333
Muromachi	1392–1573
Nanbokuchō	1337–92
Sengoku	1467–1568
Azuchi-Momoyama	1573–1600
Edo	1600–1868
Meiji	1868–1912

(Historians do not agree on exactly when the various periods started and ended, so the dates listed are approximate. Japanese writing often refers as well to nengō, or shorter periods named after each reigning emperor. Some of these will be introduced where relevant.)

Distributed in the United States by Kodansha America, Inc., 575 Lexington Avenue, New York, N.Y. 10022, and in the United Kingdom and continental Europe by Kodansha Europe Ltd., 95 Aldwych, London WC2B 4JF.

Published by Kodansha International Ltd., 17-14 Otowa 1-chome, Bunkyo-ku, Tokyo 112-8652, and Kodansha America, Inc. Copyright © 2003 Fumon Tanaka and Kodansha International Ltd. All rights reserved. Printed in Japan.

ISBN 4-7700-2898-9
First edition, 2003
03 04 05 06 07 08 09 10   10 9 8 7 6 5 4 3 2 1

www.thejapanpage.com

CONTENTS

CHAPTER 5   Kenjutsu Applications   193

CHAPTER 6   Mutō-dori Techniques   209

INTRODUCTION

History is the link between past and present, but it is also the key to the future. In this book I will introduce the world of traditional martial arts, which can be seen as a continuation of samurai culture. I shall be very happy if this work can provide readers with a deeper understanding of both bushidō (the warrior code of honor) and Japan.

Traditional martial arts are also called kobudō. Kobudō comprises a number of styles (known as ryūgi) and schools (ryūha) that were formulated in the samurai era and that are still being taught today. By studying the techniques and philosophies of these ryūgi, we perpetuate the ideas of our ancestors. Central to all ryūgi is the theme of life and death.

Bushidō teaches us to seek out what is good, and to face and fight evil. It is about survival on the battlefield through the practical techniques of fighting and killing an enemy. However, it also goes beyond this, schooling us in the arts of self-improvement.

The earliest roots of bushidō can be traced to warriors known as the Mononofu (approximately 600 B.C. to A.D. 6). The Mononofu worshipped a number of gods, and according to their beliefs it was essential to fight and destroy their enemies. They were notorious for beheading their enemies to ensure that the spirits could not return, and warriors who took heads were revered as being both strong and just.

During the early to mid-Heian period (the ninth and tenth centuries), the Japanese warriors we now know as samurai were lower-class servants to members of the nobility who were either jige (peasants) or yumitori (archers). The word "samurai" actually means "one who awaits orders." In late Heian, warriors came to be known as bushi. It was around this time that they embraced Buddhism, which taught them compassion for their opponents. This was the origin of the many ideas in bushidō that taught warriors to look for ways that would enable both themselves and their opponents to survive.

The warrior class achieved political power for the first time in the Kamakura period (1192–1333), when the seat of power moved from the imperial palace in Kyoto to the new military government at Kamakura. In this period, clan leaders fought alongside their family members and retainers in a single group called a bumon. Well-known bumon included the Genji, Heike, Fujiwara, Tachibana, and Ōtomo families. Martial arts were used in battlefield combat, and warriors developed individual styles. The resulting fighting skills and philosophies were closely guarded secrets that were passed down through families.

The end of the Kamakura period was a very unstable time, partly due to the continuous fighting between rival warrior clans. The country's problems were further compounded when the Mongols, under Kublai Khan, twice sent attacking forces against Japan in the late thirteenth century. The bushi managed to repel these attacks, but the country's economic and political situation was significantly weakened.

As internal feuding throughout the country intensified, the imperial house split into two rival lines each claiming the legitimate right to rule. One of these lines tried to seize power and restore direct imperial rule, and thereby return the nobility to the elevated status it had enjoyed during the Heian period. This attempt failed, however, and as a result, two opposing imperial courts were established in the north (Kyoto) and south (Nara). This period is thus known as the Nanbokuchō period (the Northern and Southern Courts period, 1337–1392). Both emperors had the support of a great number of warriors, and the rival sides continued to clash.

During the Heian and Kamakura periods, the main battlefield weapons were the naginata (halberd) and the nagamaki (a weapon with a long blade, combining sword and naginata). In the Nanbokuchō period, the nodachi (a very long sword, also known as ōdachi) and the yari (spear) were the weapons of choice, and it is generally accepted that fighting methods also changed during this period.

It was during the Muromachi period (1392–1573) that different styles, or ryūgi, were first officially taught. This too was an unstable time with many wars, culminating in the Sengoku period (Warring States period, 1467–1568).

The military government at Kamakura had grown weak, and rival daimyō (local feudal lords who were retainers to the shogun) clashed in power struggles. The period was also characterized by the diffusion of culture, as the daimyō began to patronize the arts.

Although the samurai-bushi's main occupation was fighting wars, during this time it was also felt that warriors should develop an element of refinement and appreciation of beauty. As fighting intensified, warriors began to aspire to a higher sense of beauty in life and death. This aesthetic was called hana (flower).

The warrior class studied from the ōchō bunka (court culture), which originated in the aesthetics of the Heian-period nobility and had further developed over several hundred years. They also studied literature, poetry, and Nō drama (called sarugaku at that time). From the Nō drama yōkyoku songs, the samurai studied singing and gained a feeling for rhythm and timing, and from the shimai dance they learned about the beauty of movement: these skills they strove to incorporate into their daily routines. They also studied philosophy through Buddhism, Mikkyō (esoteric Buddhism), and *Ekikyō* ("the I-Ching Book of Changes"). Herein lay the paradox of the samurai—on the one hand, they wanted the refinement of the nobility, but on the other they wanted to excel on the battlefield. This was the duality of the warrior's nature.

The long years of instability of the medieval era finally came to a close, and an extended era of peace arrived with the Edo period (1600–1868). The samurai-bushi enjoyed the top ranks of the social hierarchy and became a proud, military nobility. They were responsible for maintaining the peace, and also became government officials and civil servants.

Even in peacetime, the samurai sought to develop bujutsu (martial arts) and hyōhō (strategy). The samurai's mentality had developed over hundreds of years of war, but they were also keenly aware of the limitations of battlefield combat alone. Thus they strove to observe a philosophy espoused by the martial arts they practiced: "Regardless of its size, if a country adheres to fighting alone it will perish. But in times of peace it is dangerous to forget about war."

In bujutsu they strove for perfection. They created eighteen divisions in the fighting arts, including kenjutsu (sword fighting), sōjutsu (spear fighting),

bajutsu (horsemanship), kyūjutsu (archery), naginatajutsu (halberd fighting), bōjutsu (long-stick fighting), iaijutsu (fast sword-fighting), shurikenjutsu (knife throwing), juttejutsu (capturing and tying up an opponent), among others. The eighteen arts are also called "bugei jūhappan," and cover many techniques and principles developed to a very high standard.

According to Confucius, "An educated person should be well prepared for combat and will therefore surely win." The martial arts were thus accorded a cultured status and became as respected as any other field of study. bujutsu also espoused a twofold philosophy: it had to be effective in times of war, but also useful in times of peace to develop one's character and spirit. This is the essence of bun-bu-ryōdō (in which martial arts and literature were considered separate though equally important) and bun-bu-ittai (in which martial arts and literature are considered one and the same).

The essence of bushidō is death. The beauty of a warrior's existence lies in his readiness to give up his life at any time, and his physical and spiritual preparedness to take resolute action. Thus a samurai should be well-mannered and a master in martial arts, but he should never be a killer. In times of sudden danger, he should be able to see calmly the essence of all things. Possessing this kind of spirit, and striving for beauty in life and death, is central to both the samurai-bushi and to the classical martial arts as a whole.

CHAPTER 1

壱

KOBUDŌ AND THE JAPANESE SWORD

KOBUDŌ HISTORY

Jinmu Tennō, the first emperor of Japan.

Kobudō has a long history, with swords like tsurugi (with double cutting edge) and katana (single cutting edge) appearing in Japanese mythology, as recorded in works such as the *Kojiki* ("Record of Ancient Matters," 712) and *Nihon Shoki* ("Chronicle of Japan," 720). These eighth-century works were the first documented accounts of Japan's mythological age, and were based on many years of oral tradition.

According to these works, during the mythological Age of the Gods the Japanese islands were inhabited by many deities who lived as family groups or small tribes which fought amongst each other. It is said that a group using the hoko (an early type of spear) managed, through the special power of this weapon, to gather the scattered groups together and establish a small nation. They were later conquered by a group armed with bronze swords (tsurugi) as well as hoko. The resulting larger nation was known as Tsurugi no kuni ("land of the sword").

Before long another tribe appeared, led by the warrior gods Takemikazuchi-no-mikoto and Futsunushi-no-mikoto, who were armed with iron swords called Futsunomitama-no-tsurugi ("swords of spiritual power"). They met with Ōkuninushi-no-mikoto, king of Tsurugi no Kuni, on the beach, where they each thrust their Futsunomitama-no-tsurugi into the sand and ordered the king to surrender his country to the sun goddess Amaterasu Ōmi-no-kami. The king feared the power of their swords, and so ceded his land. Takemikazuchi-no-mikoto and Futsunushi-no-mikoto are still today considered the guardian deities of the traditional martial arts.

Ancient samurai, known as Mononofu, date back 2500 to 3000 years.

Mononofu with their main weapon, the bow and arrow.

Prince Shōtoku was prince regent to Empress Suiko (r. 592–628). He governed in her place as a warrior and a statesman, and was an influential member of the aristocracy.

Prince Shōtoku, who defeated the Mononofu and ruled the country according to Buddhist philosophy, promulgated the Seventeen-Article Constitution, and established the Kan-i-jūnikai (twelve court ranks).

The first emperor of Japan was the great-great-grandson of the sun goddess Amaterasu Ōmi-no-kami. As a god he was called Kamuyamatoiwarebi-no-mikoto, but after he became emperor he was known as Jinmu Tennō. Having united several small nations in the southern island of Kyūshū, Kamuyamatoiwarebi-no-mikoto advanced with his army to central Japan. However, he met fierce opposition from the local armies and his elder brother Sano-no-mikoto was killed, after which his soldiers lost the will to fight. At that moment, the god Takakuraji-no-mikoto gave him the Futsunomitama-no-tsurugi originally owned by Takemikazuchi-no-mikoto, telling him it was a gift from heaven in order to help him win. As Kamuyamatoiwarebi-no-mikoto drew the sword, he and his soldiers felt its divine power and they thus regained their strength. So it was that they were victorious and Kamuyamatoiwarebi-no-mikoto became Emperor Jinmu in 1600 B.C.

The Futsunomitama-no-tsurugi therefore came to be worshipped as a divine sword. Warriors at the time were called Mononofu, and in combat they uttered magic words while holding a shield in their left hand and a tsurugi or hoko in their right.

In the sixth century, Buddhism was introduced into Japan. This was in the reign of the thirty-third emperor, Shōtoku Taishi (574–622), prince

Genpei-no-kassen. Two powerful bushi clans, the Genji and Heike, fought many fierce battles. This picture shows a scene from the final battle, in which the Genji general Minamoto no Yoshitsune rides into the sea to retrieve his bow.

The battle of Chihaya-Akasaka in the Nanbokuchō period.

Shogun Ashikaga Takauji, who became shogun at the end of the Nanbokuchō period, boards his ship on his way to battle.

Bushi in classical one-on-one combat on horseback. Before a duel, a bushi would follow accepted protocol by calling out his name to his opponent.

Bushi scouts lighting warning fires to signal the approach of an enemy.

regent to empress Suiko (r. 593–628). Prince Shōtoku was devoutly Buddhist, and was also a great martial arts master. His army fought with rival Mononofu clans, who followed the traditional Shinto beliefs. Prince Shōtoku's forces emerged the victors and Shōtoku ruled the country according to Buddhist philosophy. He established twelve court ranks, and promulgated the Seventeen-Article Constitution, which specified how people should live their lives. Prince Shōtoku thus laid the foundations for a peaceful and orderly political state that accepted both Shinto and Buddhist beliefs. From this time martial arts practitioners started to study the philosophies of both Shinto and Buddhism.

For most of the Heian period, the imperial court and the nobility in Kyoto governed the country. At that time the bushi were farmers and foresters, and only in times of war did they leave their fields to fight using bow and arrow

Portrait of warrior-general Kusunoki Masashige (?–1336), whose brilliance in battle made him a hero durring the Nanbokuchō period.

Picture of a warrior with a nodachi (or ōdachi, a very long sword) in his hand. Bushi wore a medium length sword known as a chūdachi which hung at their side on laces called sageo. They wore two further short swords—a wakizashi (on their left side) and a metezashi (on their right side)—bringing the total number of swords they wore into battle to four.

Tengu (mythical creatures with a long beak and wings living deep in the mountains). It was often said that a bushi who was particularly skilled in swordsmanship was trained by these creatures.

The author with a nodachi.

or sword. Some of the bushi were employed by the nobility as guards or soldiers, but were of such low rank that they were not allowed to enter the palace. They were referred to as jige, and had to kneel on the ground while awaiting their orders. From that time the word "samurai" was coined, deriving from "saburomono," meaning "he who awaits orders."

By the end of the Heian period, noted for its prolonged years of peace and highly refined court culture, the absence of a centralized military system in the ranks of the nobility had allowed the provincial warrior families to assume more power. Some bushi stopped following the orders of the nobility in Kyoto altogether, and fighting spread as rivalries intensified.

The Genji and the Heike emerged as the most powerful warrior clans, and as both had imperial blood they presented a challenge to the imperial rule. The struggle for power between the Genji and the Heike led to fighting

Spears or long sticks of iron were frequently used on the battlefield.

The great warlord Takeda Shingen (1521–1573) and his twenty-three military commanders. They were the most prominent bushi horsemen in the Sengoku period.

① ②

Nōgaku (Nō drama). Bushi became military nobles after the Sengoku period (1467–1568). Nō drama, one of Japan's oldest traditional performing arts, became an important focus of cultural study for the bushi. The principle actors wear marks and lavish costumes, which denote conventional categories such as gods, priests, and demons, and the intricate, precise choreography of their movements denotes the characters' emotions and inner spirits. This picture shows one of the most famous Nō dramas, *Tamura* ①. In 2001, Nōgaku was designated as a World Heritage by UNESCO.

Chūjōhime ②, the princess heroine of the Nō drama *Hibariyama*, who for many years bears her cruel stepmother's ill treatment of her without complaint and eventually becomes a nun in a mountain hermitage.

The Nō drama *Tsuchigumo* ("Earth Spider") ③. This scene reproduces the fight between Minamoto no Yorimitsu (also known as Raikō, 948–1021), and the mythical monster Tsuchigumo. This picture depicts Tsuchigumo spinning its thread to ensnare the warrior.

③

throughout the country, known as Genpei no kassen (Heike-Genji conflict, 1180–1185). The Genji eventually defeated and completely destroyed the Heike in 1185.

In 1192 the leader of the Genji, Minamoto no Yoritomo, established a military government at Kamakura and thus reduced the imperial court in Kyoto to symbolic status. It is from this time that the real warrior era started as the bushi began to enjoy a higher social status. This lasted for 676 years, until the Meiji Restoration in 1868 when the samurai were stripped of their titles and rank.

Samurai prayed to the gods of budō for good fortune in battle.

Fudō Myōō (the god of fire).

Mari Shiten (the god of self-defence and victory).

Batō Kannon (the bodhisattva Kannon with the head of a horse).

The Kamakura period (1185–1333) was characterized by incessant fighting, starting with the clash between Minamoto no Yoritomo and his brother Minamoto no Yoshitsune. This was followed by the Jōkyū no ran (Jōkyū Disturbance, 1221), when the emperor's forces attempted unsuccessfully to depose the Kamakura government, as well as various other conflicts and the Mongol invasions in 1274 and 1281. Fighting skills and the quality of weapons such as the sword, spear, halberd, and nagamaki (long sword), accordingly underwent major improvements during this period.

Instability and conflict continued during the Muromachi period (1333–1573), in which it was not unheard-of for shogun to be slain by their own retainers. In Kyoto, the city of the emperor's palace, the protracted Ōnin no ran (Ōnin War, 1467–1477) marked the onset of the Sengoku (Warring States) period.

The Sengoku period came to an end when the general Toyotomi Hideyoshi (1537–1598) finally managed to unify the nation. He was succeeded by Tokugawa Ieyasu (1543–1616), who became shogun and moved the seat of government to Edo (modern-day Tokyo) in 1603. Ieyasu established a political system that made the Tokugawa family the leader of all samurai throughout Japan, in order to exert increased control over provincial daimyō and preclude power struggles.

During the Edo period, Japan pursued an isolationist policy, having contact only with Holland, China, and Korea. During the extended period of peace, bushidō became highly accomplished, as fighting techniques, spirit, and philosophy were thoroughly researched and refined. The bujutsu and ryūgi developed during this period have been handed down to the present day.

CLASSICAL
AND MODERN BUDŌ

Hirokazu Kanazawa, president of the Shōtō-kan Karatedō International Federation, and one of the most renowned karate masters in the world.

There are two kinds of budō in Japan today. Those budō forms that have a long tradition, and were closely associated with bushidō, are called kobudō, or classical budō. Those formulated after the samurai era ended in 1868 are called gendai budō, or modern budō; often also called sports budō. Kobudō has a history dating back to the mythological period. Throughout Japan's history, with its many wars, various martial arts were developed, including jūjutsu, kenjutsu, sōjutsu, naginatajutsu, kyūjutsu, bōjutsu, hanbōjutsu (half-length bōjutsu), shuri-kenjutsu, torinawajutsu (capturing and binding using a rope), juttejutsu, and ninjutsu (ninja technique), among others. Collectively they are known as bugei jūhappan ("the eighteen martial arts") and taught either individually as single disciplines, or in combination to form an overall discipline. Within each of the eighteen martial arts, various styles (ryūgi) evolved, and these styles were taught in traditional schools (ryūha), many of which still exist today.

Some kobudō techniques are based on real combat experience and others on Buddhism, Shinto, or ancient Chinese philosophy. Kobudō also emphasizes the importance of etiquette, manners, and ceremony, which are carefully adhered to in each ryūha. Students must develop their body and mind, and should preserve the art within their family. This tradition has been maintained for many hundreds of years. Students who have mastered the technical and philosophical side of the ryūha receive a licence called menkyo kaiden from their teacher. This licence is usually in the form of a makimono (scroll). A ryūha has only one sōke (head of the school), but can have several shihanke, or shihan—students

Toshihisa Sofue, who has won the Karatedō School Teachers' Tournament many times.

Shigenobu Ogino, shihan of the JR Nishi Nihon Kendō Federation. He often practices and teaches wearing a white keikogi (practice uniform) and white hakama (divided skirt).

Kendō equipment.

JR Nishi Nihon Kendō Federation high-ranking dan group. Shihan Ogino sits in the front row, center.

of the sōke who have themselves become masters and taken on students.

Gendai budō includes some seven methods: jūdō, kendō, naginatadō, karatedō, aikidō, Shōrinji kenpō, and jūkendō.

Judō, which became an Olympic discipline in 1964, was developed by Kanō Jigorō and his students. It is a sport based on classical jūjutsu, from which atemi (body strikes), metsubushi (attack to the eyes), kyūsho (attack to vulnerable parts of the body), the use of hidden weapons, and other dangerous techniques that can injure or kill an opponent have been removed.

Kendō and naginatadō are sports that use protective clothing and safety weapons. In kendō, a bamboo safety sword called a shinai is used. In naginatadō, a bamboo shinai naginata is used. Both of these modern budō place emphasis on etiquette and manners, and also teach the bushidō spirit.

Kendō technique starting from sonkyo (squatting position).

Kendō technique starting from seigan ("aiming-at-the-eye") posture).

Frontal attack to the opponent's *men* (front of the head) from seigan.

Kendō's short-sword kata.

Karate was a traditional martial art from Okinawa, which until four hundred years ago was independent from Japan and was known as the Ryūkyū Kingdom. Ryūkyū became the prefecture of Okinawa in the Meiji period (1868–1912). In karate there are several styles, such as Shitō Ryū, and Gōjū Ryū, but these styles were developed in Japan from the late Meiji until the Shōwa period (1926–1989).

Aikidō and Shōrinji kenpō are not fighting techniques created to defeat an opponent, but methods using budō principles to develop the mind and body of the practitioners.

Originally jūkendō came to Japan from France around the end of the Edo period. It was developed during the Meiji period, when techniques based on Japanese classical spear fighting were integrated. It became an essential art for soldiers, but was also practiced as a sport by ordinary people.

Kobudō upholds the tradition from the samurai era and is handed down in the form of makimono. This photograph shows the makimono of four of the ryūha of which Fumon Tanaka is the inheritor.

Kobudō's menkyo makimono contain not only martial arts techniques but also secrets of magic spells, fortune-telling (astrology), battle formation, and ninjutsu.

A major difference between kobudō and gendai budō is in the method of licensing. Kobudō uses the menkyo (licences) system whereby licenses are awarded by masters to students in the form of makimono. These include shoden (basic level), chūden (intermediate level), okuden (master's level), and kaiden (deep initiation): students who rise through all of these are called menkyo kaiden. The descendants of a menkyo kaiden, regardless of whether they are actual blood relatives or not, can succeed him as the inheritor of the tradition on condition that they have mastered all the practical and philosophical teachings.

Gendai budō issues nine dan grades from shodan (1st dan) to kyūdan (9th dan), and further awards the ranks renshi (high), kyōshi (second highest), and hanshi (highest). Grades and ranks are awarded only to the person who accomplishes them, and cannot be passed on to descendants.

JŪJUTSU

①

②

③

Jūjutsu, also known as kumiuchi, yawara, and kenpō, is the basis of all martial arts. It is the fighting art with which one stops an opponent's attack without using weapons, and also includes counterattacks and methods to immobilize an opponent. Toward the end of the Sengoku period, it was considered proof of great skill to capture an opponent alive, and warriors who did this were appraised very highly by their superiors. Jūjutsu was therefore an essential skill for warriors on the battlefield. From the Edo period, jūjutsu was used by the police to capture criminals, and it also became a method of self-defense for commoners.

This highly skilled art has been preserved until today. *Classical Fighting Arts of Japan: A Complete Guide to Koryū Jūjutsu* (Kodansha International, 2001), which was written by my student Serge Mol, introduces the history of jūjutsu in great detail and is recommended literature for anyone wanting to know more about this traditional art.

HANKAKE-NAGE
Both parties start from a standing position ①. The party on the right attacks with a punch to the face ②. The party on the left blocks the attack ③, counterattacks, and throws the attacker over her shoulder ④.

④

Tentsuki (atemiwaza, striking technique).

Ashinata (immobilization).

Kannuki (katamewaza, grappling technique).

Kata guruma (nagewaza, throwing technique).

Portrait of Zen priest Takeda Butsuge on his way to a festival, carrying a heavy temple bell weighing more than 200 kg. The founder of Fusen Ryū Jūjutsu, he was famous for his strength.

① ②

③

UCHIKOMI DORI

Both parties start from seiza (formal sitting position) ①. The party on the right attacks with a hammerfist strike ②. The party on the left blocks the attack and immobilizes his attacker with an armlock ③.

①

②

③

④

⑤

ICHIMONJI

Both parties start from seiza ①. The party on the left takes the initiative and kicks his opponent in the chest ②. The opponent falls backward ③, and is choked when he tries to get up ④–⑤.

①

②

③

④

SAKAKESA

Both parties start from a standing position ①. The party on the left attacks with a punch to the face ②. The party on the right blocks the attack, moves in ③, and chokes his attacker ④.

SHINDŌ TENSHIN RYŪ'S HISHIGI TORITEJUTSU

Both parties start from a standing position ①. The party on the left attacks with a knife slash ②. The party on the right blocks the attack by hitting his attacker's forearm with a short stick ③–④. Next, he controls the arm ⑤, moves in ⑥, and chokes his attacker with the short stick ⑦.

Demonstrated by sōke Tenshin Kaminaga and inheritor Hisashi Kaminaga.

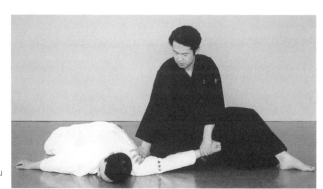

Kohaku Iwai, shike of the Kanra-kiraku Ryū, demonstrating an armlock.

KENJUTSU

The Japanese sword (nihontō) is deeply bound to Japanese history. Traditionally seen as the soul of the warrior, it was believed to possess divine power. For these reasons, kenjutsu, the art of sword fighting, is one of the most highly respected martial arts.

Kenjutsu is based on battlefield experience and practices developed by individual warriors. Educated warriors of the highest rank always carried a sword, and they studied kenjutsu above any other martial art.

KODEN ENSHIN RYŪ'S KENJUTSU KIRIAGE

Both swordsmen start from hassō-no-kamae (the sword is held in high position with the hilt level with the right shoulder) ①. The swordsmen each attack with two cuts at their opponent (kiriai) ②–④. After his second cut, the swordsman on the right sweeps his opponent's sword to the side ⑤. The swordsman on the left immediately assumes a posture that allows him to counterattack ⑥. The swordsman on the right moves in for a frontal attack on the left swordsman ⑦–⑧, who steps out of the line of attack slightly, and makes a cut to his opponent's temple ⑨–⑩.

SHINKAGE RYŪ'S KENJUTSU SUNDOME

When demonstrating kenjutsu, the swordsman raises his sword and brings it down as if he or she really intends to cut the opponent, but the blade must stop just before touching the opponent's body. This is called sundome, and it is the most difficult and important technique to master. This picture shows sōke Kazutora Toyoshima and shihan Tomoo Koide. Both are renowned swordsmen in Japan.

⑨

⑩

①

②

③

④

KODEN ENSHIN RYŪ'S KENJUTSU KASUMIGIRI

The swordsman on the right assumes hassō-no-kamae, the one on the left chūdan-no-kamae (middle position) ①. As the swordsman on the right prepares to attack, he is countered by his opponent, who makes a cut to his right hand ②. As the swordsman on the right continues his downward cut, his opponent steps to the left ③, and makes a cut to his neck ④.

THE HISTORY OF
THE JAPANESE SWORD

An ancient tsurugi dating from the bronze age. The surface of the blade is decorated with gold and silver shamanistic symbols. This kind of tsurugi was used in religious rituals.

The tsurugi shown here is made of iron and has two cutting edges. It was used by shamans and believed to have divine power.

Throughout Japan's history, the sword has undergone many changes, and its shape has evolved to accommodate the fighting styles of each age. Although it was essentially a weapon, it was also used in shamanistic rituals and considered a work of art.

According to historical records, from mythological times swords were called tsurugi. The body of the tsurugi was straight, with two cutting edges. For many years, the tsurugi was used in battle, and all swords used to kill and behead an enemy were believed to be imbued with divine power. They were worshipped as gods and used in shamanistic ritual. The tsurugi was originally made of stone, and later of bronze and then iron. Although the materials changed according to the age, the shape remained the same until the start of the iron age (approximately 4 B.C.), when iron swords began to be made with a straight body and a single cutting edge. These swords were called katakiriba, and later kataha. The term used today—katana—appears in documents from the sixth century. From the Nara period, the katana became a symbol of authority and divine power and thus came to represent the soul of the nobility at the imperial court, believed to be descended from the gods.

Another important, though rare, style of sword was the kuttō. This came with a single cutting edge on the inside of the curvature. The Futsunomitama-no-tsurugi that, according to Japanese mythology, possessed divine powers and was responsible for the unification of Japan, is the first and most famous of these swords. It is believed that over two thousand years ago, Futsunomitama-no-tsurugi was placed in a stone box and buried in the sacred ground of a shrine at Isonokami,

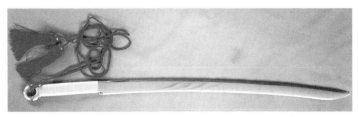

A replica of Futsunomitama-no-tsurugi, the sword possessed by the gods Take-mikazuchi-no-mikoto and Futsunushi-no-mikoto, today revered as the guardian deities of the martial arts. This type of curved sword, with the cutting edge on the inside of the curvature, is called a kuttō.

Katakiriba-no-tsurugi. The katakiriba, also called kataha, was a symbol of power for the ancient nobility.

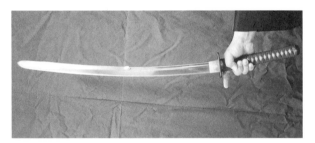

A kogarasumaru sword with two cutting edges extending about half the length of the curved blade. This sword is a replica of a blade made by Amakuni, who is considered the guardian deity of swordsmiths.

The style of sword known as jindachi was designed specifically for use on the battlefield. The sword shown here was used by a daimyō (feudal lord) at formal ceremonies during the largely peaceful Edo period, when jindachi assumed a more symbolic role.

in Yamato (the present-day city of Tenri, in Nara prefecture). In 1874, a ceremony was held to exhume the sword for maintenance, after which it was reinterred. Futsunomitama-no-tsurugi is considered to be a divine treasure and it is forbidden for anybody to see it.

A style that differed from the kuttō, and most likely emerged in the Nara period, was the kogarasumaru. A cutting edge was added to the outside of the blade, and both cutting edges extended about half the length of the body of the sword. The most famous surviving example of this style of sword is kept as an imperial treasure.

Later the design was again modified, with a single cutting edge extending the full length of the outside of the curvature. This katana was the preferred sword of the bushi during the Heian and Kamakura periods, when fighting

The famous warrior-general Kusunoki Masashige (?–1336). An important general would wrap the scabbard of his jindachi with the skin of a tiger or panther, seen here at his left hip, as a symbol of certain victory before going into combat.

Jindachi.

A katana, typical of the type worn by samurai during the Edo period.

Yoroi-dōshi. These swords were made for thrusting into an enemy's body through gaps in the armor (yoroi) when using kumiuchi (jūjutsu) techniques on the battlefield.

was one-on-one. These swords, however, often broke or warped in combat. When the Mongols invaded in 1331 it became clear that flaws in the design made it unsuitable for group combat. Many swordsmiths of the time worked to develop a stronger sword, but it was Masamune who invented the forging techniques still used today.

Masamune discovered that the use of just one type of steel was inadequate in the construction of a sword. Instead he used a softer steel known as shingane for the core of the blade, and covered this with the harder steel known as kawagane. Swords forged in this style rarely broke or warped, even in heavy fighting, and were thus considered the perfect weapon. Even today this weapon represents the soul of the bushi.

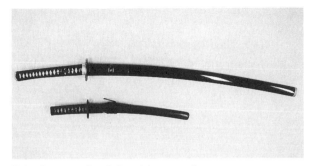

Daitō (long sword) and shōtō (short sword).

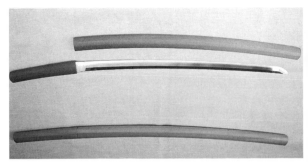

Shirasaya shikomi. The shirasaya (plain scabbard) and tsuka (hilt) are unlacquered, thereby allowing the wood to breathe and preventing the sword from rusting.

Ōdachi (nodachi). Ōdachi means "long sword," and nodachi translates as "field sword." This was the main weapon on the battlefield from the Nanbokuchō through the Sengoku periods.

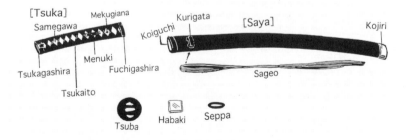

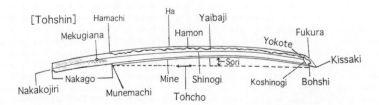

Diagram showing the parts of the katana.

THE CREATION OF
THE JAPANESE SWORD

The Japanese sword is closely linked to the spirit of bushidō and Japanese history. The sword is also a work of art, created with fire, iron, and water.

The process of its creation is rooted in Japanese folklore. The ancient people of Japan believed the activity of volcanos to be the work of the gods. From the eruptions of underwater volcanos an island emerged, and on it a prince was born. The prince was descended from the gods and possessed divine power. The ancient people also believed that the sword's creation in the forge could be likened to the divine creation of the prince; the sword too being rendered from earth, fire, and water. So it was that the sword came to be seen as sacred and infused with godly powers.

The swordsmith wears the white robes of a Shinto priest. Firstly, he purifies his body with water, and prays to the gods to purify his mind. He then channels all his spiritual and physical strength into forging the sword. The resulting blade will have the natural beauty of a waterfall, and the pattern along its edge will resemble mist hanging in a remote valley.

FORGING THE JAPANESE SWORD

Iron ore gathered from the mountains.

A tatara, or clay smelter, in operation. A tatara is used to convert raw materials into the starting steel needed for the sword.

Smelting the iron ore at high temperatures. This swordsmith wears the white robes of a Shinto priest.

The mass of smelted iron ore and carbon from the charcoal flows from the tatara, resembling the eruption of a volcano.

In the next stage, the walls of the tatara are broken apart, so that the large block of smelted steel, known as kera, which has accumulated at the bottom of the tatara, can be retrieved.

The kera block.

The kera is taken outside the tatara building using logs called koro, and is left to cool.

Close-up view of the kera after it has been broken into smaller pieces.

The kera is broken into yet smaller pieces, and separated from zuku, pig iron that contains too many impurities to be used in forging a sword.

The kera that is used to make swords is called tamahagane.

Tsumiwakashi. Using a high-temperature charcoal fire, the tamahagane is formed into small steel wafers called kōwari. These are stacked and welded to a steel bar.

The stack of kōwari is then wrapped with Japanese washi paper and coated with a clay slurry, onto which straw ash and charcoal powder are applied.

Some of the specially prepared clay slurry is dried and preserved for later use.

The wrapped and coated stack of kōwari is then heated in a charcoal fire.

When heated to high temperatures, the lump of steel glows yellow, at which point it is hammered and forged into a small block by the swordsmith and his assistants.

The swordsmith makes a deep cleft into the small block with a cutting tool known as a tagane.

Next the block is hammered down and folded over.

The block, after a cleft has been made with the tagane.

The folded-over block.

The block is forged and gradually elongated into a steel bar with a square cross-section.

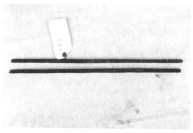

Two bars made following the above process.

Stack made up of cut sections of the steel bar.

The stack is then coated with a clay slurry and straw ash, after which it is fired to a high temperature in a charcoal furnace, and again hammered into a steel block.

The steel block with a cleft.

The folded-over block.

Detail of sword blade construction. The method used here is called kobuse gitae. A core of softer shingane (core steel) is sandwiched between a U-shaped jacket of harder kawagane (jacket steel).

Detail of the reverse side that will become the back of the sword.

Detail of the surface that will become the cutting edge of the sword.

Cross-section of a blade made using kōbuse gitae, in which a piece of kawagane steel is partially wrapped around the shingane.

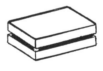

Makuri gitae. This is similar to kōbuse gitae, but in this case the shingane is completely enclosed by a single jacket of kawagane.

Detail of the reverse side of the makuri gitae.

Shihō-tsume gitae. In this method, the softer shingane core is completely surrounded by four strips of kawagane.

With the shihō-tsume method, the complete outer surface is made of hard kawagane, so any side can be used to make the cutting edge. This shows a diagram of a cross-section of this construction.

Detail of the hon sanmai (also called sanmai gitae) method. In this case, a layer of softer shingane is sandwiched between two layers of kawagane.

Hon sanmai seen from a different angle. The harder kawagane will be forged to make the cutting edge of the sword.

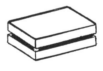

Drawing of the layers in hon sanmai.

Kawagane and shingane being forged together.

A small block of steel made using the shihō-tsume method is divided in two.

After the kawagane and shingane have been welded together, the block of steel is hammered and shaped into a bar.

Detail of the joint where the shaped bar is welded to another bar called tekogane that will serve as a handle when forging. Later this handle will be removed.

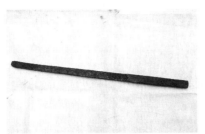

The flat bar after being removed from the tekogane. This is called the sunobe (blank shape).

Arabi-zukuri. The flat bar has been forged and shaped to the desired length. What looks like the tip and the cutting edge here is actually the part that will become the blunt edge of the blade.

After arabi-zukuri, the blade is heated again. At the section which will become the tip, or kissaki, the harder kawagane is hammered into a sharp point. This process is called hi-zukuri, or rough shaping.

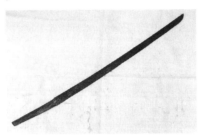

The blade after arabi-zukuri and hi-zukuri. It now has the shape of a sword, but its surface is still very rough.

The workspace and tools used to smooth and carve the blade. The tools are called sensuki.

Carving and smoothing the surface of the blade.

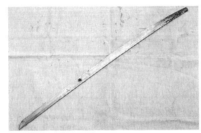

The blade after it has been carved. Next, the sword will be filed to give it an even surface.

The sword just before tsuchioki, the application of a clay coating that will harden the edge. The way the paste is applied will determine the pattern along the hamon (cutting edge).

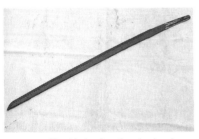

The blade after the clay has been applied.

Section of the blade near the hilt after tsuchioki.

Section of the blade near the tip after tsuchioki.

e
d
c
b
a

Different stages of forging, from bottom to top. The blade is hammered into the desired length (the sunobe, a). Next, arabi-zukuri; a shinogi, or ridge line along the side of the blade, is hammered in (b). This is followed by hi-zukuri, when the tip is hammered into a rough shape (c). (d) shows the sword after it has been carved and smoothed with sen-suki, and after filing. (e) shows the blade after tsuchioki.

The shapes of the tip at different stages of forging, from left to right.

After tsuchioki, the sword is ready for yakiire, or heat treating. The smith here is using bellows to bring the charcoal to the right temperature.

When the charcoal fire is at the right temperature, the smith picks up the sword and puts it into the forge.

The charcoal fire in the forge, at high temperature.

After the blade has been heated to the right temperature, it is plunged into a water-filled trough.

After yakiire heat treatment, the smith polishes the blade and checks its condition. This process is called kaji-oshi, or rough polishing.

If the condition of the sword after kaji-oshi is satisfactory, the smith then makes diagonal file marks on the tang.

The swordsmith then chisels his name onto the tang.

Swordsmith Kanetoki Kojima and his son Kanemichi.

CHAPTER 2

SAMURAI TRADITION

SAMURAI ATTIRE

Samurai attire: kariginu (right) and montsuki hakama (left).

I n the early Edo period bushidō was fully developed and reached the form widely recognized today. Edo society was shaped by a very strict social hierarchy, and the samurai occupied the highest ranks of the system.

When a warrior left the confines of a castle he always wore two swords—the daitō (long sword) and the shōtō (short sword). Commoners were not generally allowed to wear swords, although the shogunate allowed them to wear just one sword when traveling or holding certain ceremonies. There are several reasons why a samurai wore two swords. First of all, he had to be prepared to deal with an enemy, a sudden threat, or imminent danger at any time. Secondly, under the orders of his lord he was also expected to carry out jōiuchi, or execution of criminals. He could also be expected to conduct kaishaku (ritual beheading), to assist a samurai committing seppuku (the ritual taking of one's life; also called hara-kiri).

When a samurai had made a serious mistake he could commit seppuku using his short sword in atonement for his actions. In addition, it was considered dishonorable for a samurai to be taken alive by an enemy, and at such a time he would cut either his belly or his throat. The kaishaku practitioner assisted the seppuku ritual by cutting the samurai's neck as soon as the samurai had plunged his dagger into his own belly and blood had become visible; at that moment officials witnessing the seppuku would give a signal to the kaishaku practitioner. This was done to spare the samurai from agony, and prevent him from dishonoring himself.

A further reason for carrying two swords was so that a warrior whose spear, main sword, and other weapons had

The kariginu was worn by warriors for formal ceremonies from the Yamato period (645–710). Some warriors who were also Shinto priests wore this style of clothing until the Sengoku period.

Attire worn by young warriors in the medieval period (1192–1573).

An early name for warriors was yumitori (archer), who carried a tachi (sword) as well as bow and arrows. The clothing shown here is from the Kamakura to Nanbokuchō periods.

Famous warrior-general Minamoto no Yoshiie (1039-1106), on horseback, wearing armor and a kabuto (helmet). He is carring arrows and a long bow and is headed for battle. In this famous scene, he has noticed his enemies hiding in the field because he sees birds rising in the air.

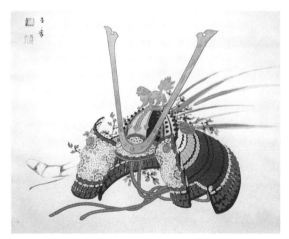

The kabuto (helmet) was said to be the most beautiful part of samurai armor at its most elaborate.

been broken in battle, and who had come to the end of his physical strength, could remove his short sword and hand it over to the enemy as a sign of his surrender. By wearing the daitō and shōtō, therefore, a warrior not only demonstrated his resolution but also accepted responsibility for his actions and pledged to live his life in honor. In many modern budō, for example iai, practitioners often wear just one sword, but these forms are not based on bushidō.

Warrior praying to his ancestors, gods, and Buddhas before going into combat. In this drawing he is wearing the hitatare above his armor, and kosode (small-cuffed kimono) inside.

While clad in armor, but not engaged in combat, warriors wore a long black cap, or kazaori eboshi, in place of the helmet.

When it was necessary to observe correct etiquette, a samurai would keep his hands tucked inside his hakama when seated.

The way that a samurai would have dressed when he went out on official business, including the jingasa helmet decorated with his family's crest (kamon).

A samurai had formal and informal attire. When going to battle, he wore yoroi (armor) over his hitatare (everyday attire which could also be worn in formal circumstances). When on duty in the castle, in public places, or at formal ceremonies, he wore kamishimo (formal wear). In his private time, he wore kimono with hakama (divided skirt), over which he could wear a haori (coat). A high ranking warrior or a lord wore a special costume, called eboshi daimon, when attending ceremonies.

EXAMPLES OF KAMON (FAMILY CRESTS)

Kamishimo clothing. In the Edo period, samurai were also government officials. The kamishimo was worn by samurai on duty.

Attire from the Edo period worn by samurai when practicing martial arts.

Montsuki-haori-hakama. When a samurai went outdoors he would always wear clothes adorned with his family crest.

A warrior's clothing was called montsuki, because it was decorated with the kamon (family crest); "mon" means "crest" and "tsuki" means "attached." By wearing this crest, the samurai was also wearing his family honor, including that of his ancestors, and so was prevented from doing anything dishonorable.

SEPPUKU AND KAISHAKU

SHINI-SHŌZOKU
The samurai committing seppuku would wear a white kimono and white hakama with no markings, known as shini-shōzoku ("shini" means "death," "shōzoku" means "costume").

Seppuku should never be considered suicide, and similarly kaishaku should never be regarded as murder: both are rituals of bushidō. Seppuku was committed only by warriors—commoners were deemed unworthy. There were several circumstances under which seppuku was carried out. One was to take personal responsibility for a grave error. A samurai would also commit seppuku if his lord commanded him to do so. A further reason would be to take responsibility for someone else's crime or error. In many cases, however, seppuku was carried out in combat when defeat was unavoidable or had already occurred. A samurai could also commit seppuku after losing in battle to ensure that the lives of his wife, children, and retainers would be spared.

Kaishaku was performed to assist the warrior committing seppuku. There were two types of kaishaku. The first was done to a samurai who had committed a crime: his head would be cut off completely. The second was done to a samurai who had not dishonored his status: a small section of skin at the front of his neck was left intact, so that his head would fall forward onto his arms while remaining attached to his neck, thus preserving his dignity. This was called "kakae-kubi."

The kaishaku practitioner would stand to the left of and behind of the person comitting seppuku, and from hassō-no-kamae, cut the samurai's head off.

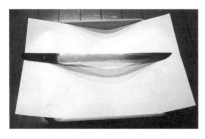

SEPPUKU-TŌ
The blade used by samurai performing seppuku was called a seppuku-tō. The most common type was a hirazukuri-yoroi-dōshi (an armor-piercing dagger with no ridgeline).The length of a blade used for seppuku was generally about 29cm.

SUEMONOGIRI

Suemonogiri is often considered synonymous with tameshigiri, or a cutting test with a sword, but this is not correct. Tameshigiri was used to test the sharpness and quality of a sword: often it was carried out on dead bodies, tied-up living criminals, or bamboo straw test objects that had been secured to something. Educated or high ranking bushi did not practice tameshigiri, as it was purely a test of the sword's sharpness, and in no way a measure of the samurai's skills.

Suemonogiri performed with a kodachi (short sword); ordinarily this was done at formal ceremonies. The same technique was also used when assisting someone committing seppuku if one had no long sword at hand.

With this technique, a skilled swordsman can cut an enemy's body squarely in half. The person doing the cutting must not cut the floor or the tatami mats.

The main halls of Izumo Shrine (left) and Kashima Shrine.

The suemonogiri of Enshin Ryū was not used to test a sword, and, unlike tameshigiri, it was carried out on objects (such as bamboo and straw) that were not secured. Suemonogiri was done as a practice for kaishaku: this was necessary because any mistake while undertaking kaishaku was impermissible. Suemonogiri was also conducted to demonstrate a warrior's iaijutsu or kenjutsu skills to his lord, and in special ceremonies at the castle or shrine.

RYŪSUI (DEMONSTRATED BY SŌKE FUMON TANAKA)

The bamboo used here has a diameter of about 11 cm. If a swordsman can cut through it perfectly, then he can also cut through a human body diagonally from shoulder to armpit.

KUMIUCHI KENPŌ

K umiuchi kenpō is a combination of sword-fighting
skills and jūjutsu in battlefield combat. In this martial art, both parties use swords. Instead of drawing
his own sword, however, the party practicing kumiuchi
kenpō uses his scabbard and hilt in combination with jūjutsu
and kenjutsu techniques to defeat his opponent. Before martial arts were separated and classified into different individual arts, fighting techniques used a variety of elements that
later became separate disciplines.

①

②

③

④

⑤

Ichimonji

The swordsman on the right prepares to draw his sword ①–②. The swordsman on the left puts his right hand on the hilt of his attacker's sword ③, while the attacker continues to draw the sword. The swordsman on the left then moves behind his attacker ④, and while keeping control over the hilt of his opponent's sword, applies a choke to his throat ⑤.

①

②

Tachi-garami

The swordsman on the right attacks from daijōdan-no-kamae (the upper-most attacking position of the sword) ①. As he is about to cut down, the party on the left rushes forward, blocks his attacker's sword with his right hand, and with his left hand thrusts the hilt of his own sword into the attacker's chest ②. He then pulls his own sword out of his obi (belt) ③ and uses it to apply an armlock to the attacker's right arm ④–⑤.

③

④

⑤

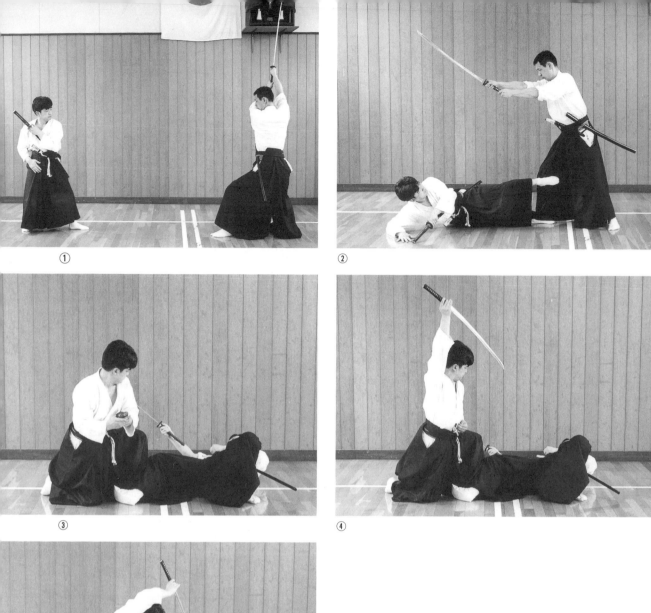

Sutemi

As the swordsman on the right attacks ①, the party on the left quickly drops to the floor ②, while counterattacking with a leg entanglement maneuver ③. As soon as the attacker has fallen down, he draws his own sword ④ and delivers the finishing stroke ⑤.

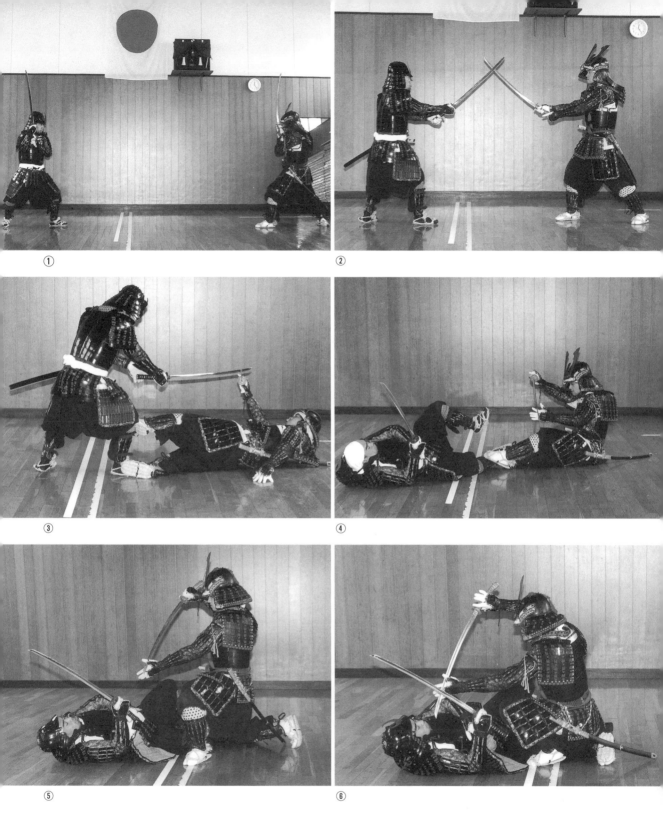

The technique shown here is exactly the same as the previous sutemi technique, only this time both swordsmen are clad in armor.

SHORT-SWORD TECHNIQUE

Depending on the length and shape of the blade, the short sword is known as either shōtō (literally, short sword), wakizashi (sub-sword, side sword) or yoroi-dōshi (an armor-piercing dagger without a ridge-line). A warrior customarily wore the daitō and the shōtō when outside. While inside a castle or at home, however, they only wore a shōtō, and therefore in the event of a sudden attack, it was necessary to be familiar with short-sword fighting techniques. On the battlefield, the short sword was especially useful against opponents armed with long weapons, such as spears, since it allowed very rapid movements.

At present there are still several schools that instruct students in the use of the short sword. One of the oldest schools teaching short-sword techniques is the Yagyū Shinkage Ryū, one of whose techniques will be introduced here.

Portrait of a tengu from the secret scroll of Yagyū Shinkage Ryū.

①

②

③

④

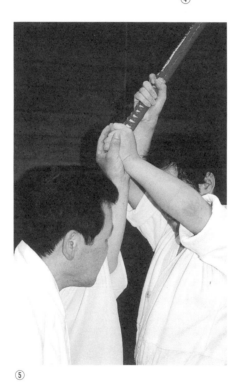

⑤

⑥

Shinkage Ryū's short-sword technique

(DEMONSTRATED BY TADASHIGE WATANABE, SŌSHU OF THE SHINKAGE RYŪ MAROBASHIKAI, AND HIS STUDENT)

The swordsman with the short sword moves slowly toward his opponent, who has assumed jōdan-no-kamae ①. As the opponent cuts down, the party on the left blocks the attack by counterattacking with his short sword ②–③. Next, he controls his attacker's hands with his left hand ④–⑤, and thrusts his short sword into the attacker's stomach ⑥.

CHAPTER 3

TWO-SWORD TECHNIQUES

THE ROOTS OF NITŌ-KEN

Old scrolls belonging to the Shinkage Ryū and Tetsujin Ryū contain similar drawings of the gods Izanami-no-kami and Izanagi-no-kami practicing kenjutsu. Izanami is using a bamboo branch in place of a sword; Izanagi is using the leaves of a tree in place of two swords, indicating that the roots of nitō-ken are extremely old.

The origin of nitō-ken (two-sword techniques) can be traced as far back as mythological times, and it is believed that the god Izanagi-no-kami invented the style. In recorded history, however, two-sword fighting began to replace the former battle technique of sword and shield that had prevailed until the end of the seventh century.

Nitō-ken was established as a martial art toward the end of the Sengoku period (1467–1568) by Miyamoto Musashi no kami Yoshimoto, grandfather of the famous samurai Miyamoto Musashi (1584?–1645). Together with a Shinto priest whose name is unrecorded because he was also a ninja, Yoshimoto formulated the Enmei Ryū martial arts school, the first to include nitō-ken techniques.

His son, Miyamoto Munisai (Miyamoto Musashi's father), studied Enmei Ryū, and from this he created another martial arts school, Tōri Ryū, with its own style of nitō-ken.

Sections of an old scroll belonging to the Musō Ryū, featuring techniques taught by Miyamoto Musashi's father, Munisai.

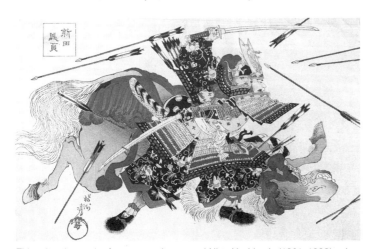

This print shows the famous warrior-general Nitta Yoshisada (1301–1338) using two swords to deflect arrows. By Yoshisada's time this was already an established form of nitō-ken.

Drawings of nitō-ken techniques in an old scroll from the Tetsujin Ryū.

Tetsujin Ryū's jitte dori technique (capturing and binding using a jitte, a hand-held weapon similar to a dagger with a long guard) uses the nitō principle. The left hand holds the jitte, the right holds the long sword.

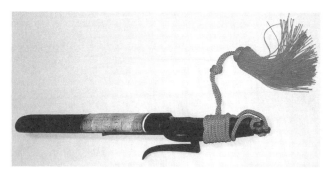

Jitte folded up and inserted in a saya (scabbard).

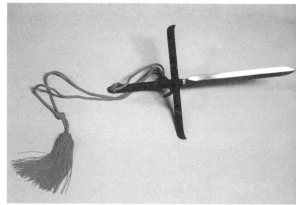

Opened and fully assembled jitte.

Over the next two centuries, nitō-ken evolved through many different schools and styles: the Tetsujin Jitte Ryū, created by Yoshimoto's younger brother, Aoki Tsuneemon, and Aoki's grandson, Aoki Tetsujin; the Musō Ryū, created by Munisai's student; and the Niten Ichi Ryū, created by Miyamoto Musashi. The nitō-ken techniques from the above schools all derived from the original Enmei Ryū style, and have been studied by a great number of people.

MIYAMOTO MUSASHI'S NITŌ-KEN

Kameo Yonehara, the ninth-generation sōke daiken of Niten Ichi Ryū.

I n the history of nitō-ken, Miyamoto Musashi is undoubtedly the most famous swordsman. He was born toward the end of the Sengoku period, and the contrast between the first and the second half of his life is quite startling.

In his early years, he was a strong and courageous fighter, a master swordsman who fought more than sixty duels without losing a single one. In the second half of his life, however, he gave up fighting and became a poet-artist, a philosopher, a brush painting artist, and a teacher. He drew plans for a new town, Akashi, that featured a classical design with traditional Japanese gardens.

In that period, he also instructed students in the secrets of kenjutsu, and wrote *Heihō Sanjūgokajō* ("The Thirty-Five Articles of Strategy") for the daimyō Hosokawa Tadatoshi (1563–1646), and later *Gorin-no-Sho* ("The Book of Five Rings") for his students, including his most trusted student Terao Motomenosuke. Just a week before his death, Musashi wrote *Dokkodō* ("The Way of Walking Alone") in which he records the twenty-one articles of his personal philosophy of life. His writings still inspire modern readers, including businessmen and managers who apply his philosophy to business.

Musashi formulated five nitō-ken kata, which he passed on to his students. These five kata are called gohō-no-kamae, and include chūdan (mid position of the sword), jōdan (upper position of the sword), gedan (lower position of the sword), migi-waki (right position of the sword), and hidari-waki (left position of the sword).

FIVE BASIC NITŌ POSTURES
(DEMONSTRATED BY NITEN ICHI RYŪ SHIHAN TOKISADA IMANISHI)

Chūdan-no-kamae

Jōdan-no-kamae

Gedan-no-kamae

Migi-waki-no-kamae

Hidari-waki-no-kamae

These techniques are still carefully preserved and taught today by the eighth generation sōke Tesshin Aoki, and his student Kameo Yonehara (the ninth generation sōke daiken). With the cooperation of shihan Imanishi (a student of Kameo Yonehara) and his student Akio Yoshimoto, the following kata are introduced in this book.

Ipponme-no-kata chūdan

Uchidachi, using ittō (one sword), assumes hassō-no-kamae; shidachi, using nitō (two swords) assumes chūdan-no-kamae. (NOTE: Uchidachi is the attacker; shidachi defends and counterattacks.)

Uchidachi makes a downward cut. Shidachi evades this attack and raises both of his swords with the tips tilted downward.

Shidachi and uchidachi both make downward cuts toward each other, but since they are too far apart, neither makes contact.

Uchidachi quickly raises his sword and attacks.

Shidachi blocks uchidachi's sword with his own short sword (left hand) and attacks uchidachi's left hand with his long sword (right hand).

Both sides assume chūdan-no-kamae and maintain zanshin (mental and physical alertness against the opponent's attack).

Final position.

Uchidachi's zanshin-no-kamae (zanshin guard position).

The Reigan cave where Miyamoto Musashi practicd Zen meditation and wrote *Gorin-no-Sho* and *Dokkodo* in his last days.

①

②

③

④

⑤

⑥

⑦ ⑧ ⑨ ⑩

Sanbonme-no-kata gedan

Uchidachi, using itō, assumes hassō-no-kamae. Shidachi, using nitō, assumes gedan-no-kamae ①. Uchidachi cuts to shidachi's head; shidachi blocks this cut by crossing his two swords ② and sweeps uchidachi's sword to the right (shidachi's right) ③.

Next, uchidachi attacks once more ④. Shidachi blocks ⑤ and sweeps uchidachi's sword again to the right ⑥.

Uchidachi attacks a third time ⑦. Shidachi parries the attack with his short sword ⑧ and sweeps it to the right ⑨, then attacks uchidachi's right upper arm with his long sword ⑩.

①　②　③　④　⑤　⑥　⑦　⑧

⑨ ⑩ ⑪ ⑫ ⑬

The tower erected for the repose of the soul of Miyamoto Musashi at Kumamoto.

Gohonme-no-kata migi-waki

Uchidachi, using ittō, assumes hassō-no-kamae ①. Shidachi, using nitō, first assumes chūdan-no-kamae, then migi-waki ②. Uchidachi attacks, and shidachi controls uchidachi's sword using the igeta form ("parallel crosses") ③–④. Shidachi raises his swords ⑤–⑥ and cuts downward ⑦. Uchidachi retreats, assumes hassō-no-kamae ⑧, and attacks again ⑨. Shidachi evades the attack by leaning backward, raises both of his swords with the tips pointing down ⑩, and parries the attack with his short sword on the left ⑪. He then counterattacks with his long sword ⑫, finishing the kata maintaining zanshin ⑬.

井

The igeta form.

SHINKAGE RYŪ'S NITŌ-YABURI

①

Yagyū Hyōgonosuke (1579–1650) was the third generation of the Yagyū-Shinkage Ryū, and was a friend of Miyamoto Musashi. Together, Hyōgonosuke and Musashi researched nitō-ken and developed techniques to counterattack and overcome nitō using only one sword. These techniques are called nitō-yaburi, and have been handed down to descendants of Hyōgonosuke. They were, however, only taught to a very select number of students. Today the correct tradition of nitō-yaburi is preserved by Tadashige Watanabe, sōshu of the Shinkage Ryū Marobashikai.

Nitō-yaburi

The nitō swordsman assumes chūdan-no-kamae ①. The ittō swordsman assumes gedan-no-kamae and slowly moves forward ②. When his opponent is close enough to attack, the ittō swordsman sweeps up the nitō swordsman's long sword ③, thus breaking his posture, and then attacks his right arm ④.

Portait of a fight between a nittō and an ittō swordsman, from the secret scroll of Yagyū Shinkage Ryū.

② ③ ④ ⑤ ⑧

YAGYŪ SHINGAN RYŪ'S NITŌ-KEN

①

②

③

The Yagyū Shingan Ryū developed many special two-sword techniques, one of which is introduced here.

Yagyū Shingan Ryū's Nitō kodachi

In traditional Japanese martial arts, it is the custom that after students complete their study, they should seek to develop new variations of their own. In Yagyū Shingan Ryū, the base of all techniques is jūjutsu, which in this ryūha is called kenpō. After students have mastered kenpō, they can start practicing sword techniques. The kata shown in the photograph is called kataginu. Only those students who have reached a high level in kenpō can carry out the nitō application of this basic technique.

Yagyū Shingan Ryū's kataginu kata deals with a situation that assumes one is sitting inside (in one's house or castle), and is suddenly grabbed by an attacker sitting in front of them ①. In this version, the person being attacked reacts with atemi (blow to the body), first to the left and then to the right ②–⑦. He then quickly draws his own short sword ⑧–⑨ and then that of his attacker ⑩–⑫. Finally, the attacker is neutralized using a nitō kodachi technique ⑬–⑮. As the technique is executed very quickly, only those who have full mastery of the basics of jūjutsu can accomplish it. The kata finishes with both parties sheathing their swords ⑯–⑲.

④

⑤ ⑥ ⑦ ⑧ ⑨ ⑩ ⑪ ⑫

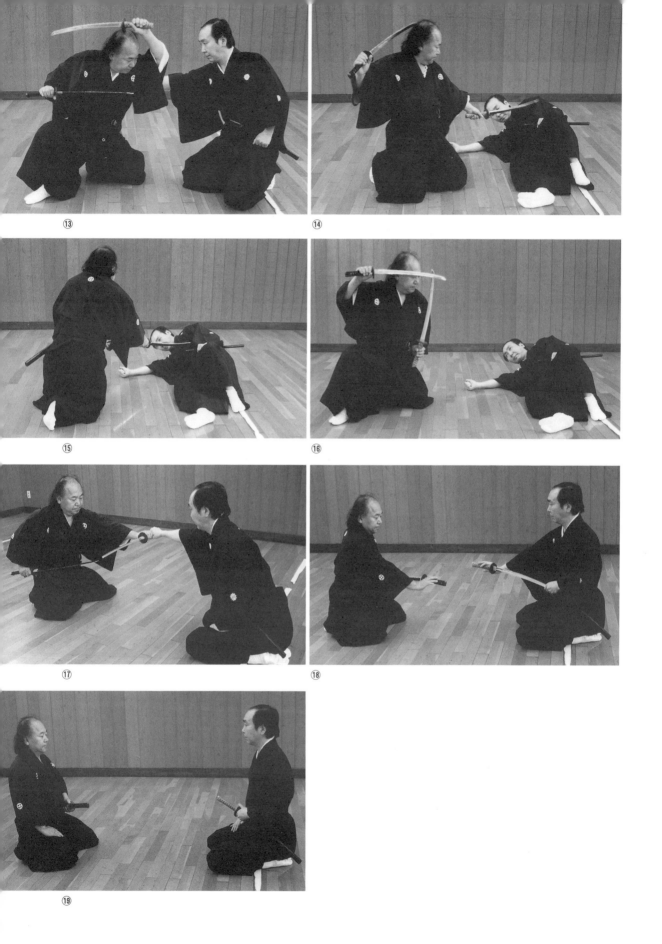

⑬　⑭

⑮　⑯

⑰　⑱

⑲

CHAPTER 4

HONMON ENSHIN RYŪ TECHNIQUES

ENSHIN RYŪ'S
IAI SUEMONOGIRI KENPŌ

Enshin Ryū's iai suemonogiri kenpō is a combination of Enshin Ryū's ancient and complex techniques as they were taught in the Edo period with other modified techniques, and with techniques of six other traditional schools. It was developed between 1915 and 1925 to make it easier for people of a new era to practice sword techniques as a curriculum.

Enshin Ryū includes jūjutsu, iai, and suemonogiri, and these three martial arts are called the san gusoku. It is essential for Enshin Ryū students to study all three of these martial arts, as it was in all traditional schools. In modern times, however, the various martial arts such as iaijutsu, jūjutsu, sōjutsu, or naginatajutsu, are often seen as individual arts and taught separately. Enshin Ryū adheres to its traditional roots and teaches these three arts together.

In Enshin Ryū, it is also important to practice kenjutsu, for without it the study of martial arts culture, which is closely associated with bushidō, would be incomplete.

The iai kenpō techniques that will be introduced here are part of the curriculum that was modified between 1915 and 1925. Nevertheless, the underlying ideas of the various techniques, the mental attitude, and the martial spirit are the same as they were in the samurai period.

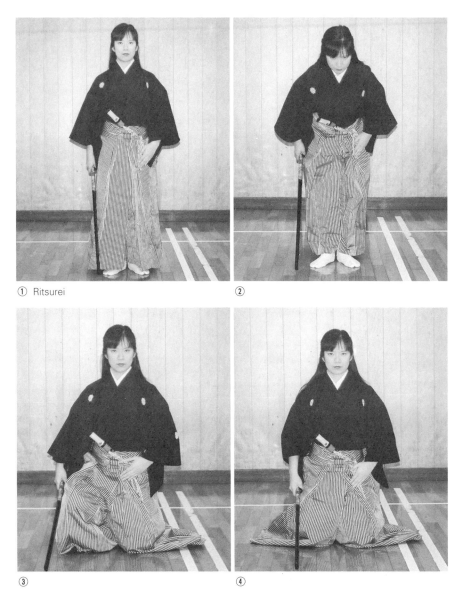

① Ritsurei ②

③ ④

Reishiki

In Japan, festivals and rites honoring the various deities have been held for over three thousand years. These were observed by the aristocracy and ordinary people alike, and became the basis of reigi (courtesy, etiquette, protocol). Bushi and the foundations of bushidō emerged some nine hundred years ago. About four hundred years later, in the Edo period, bushidō was finally established as a comprehensive warrior code. All through the history of bushidō, gishiki (ritual) and reigi (etiquette) have been carefully preserved. Even today, great emphasis is still placed on reigi based on ancient bushidō. When practicing iai, for example, we use the sword, often considered the soul of the warrior, so we regard reishiki as being of the utmost importance. Reishiki is also an important element in training. By performing reishiki, we pay our respects to the Shinto gods and the various deities of Buddhism,

⑤ Seizarei ⑥ ⑦

⑧ ⑨

⑩ ⑪

as well as to the founder of the school (the ryūso), and even to the spirit of our own sword. While improving our martial skills, we seek to develop our personality, common sense, and strong willpower, under the protection of the gods and Buddhas.

⑫

⑬

⑭

⑮

⑯

⑰

⑱

⑲

⑳ Tōrei

㉑

㉒

㉓

㉔

㉕

㉖

㉗ Uyamai
Saluting the katana, which is a divine object.

㉘

㉙

㉚

㉛

㉜ Taitō

㉝

㉞

㉟

㊱ Ōshin-no-kamae

① ② ③

④ ⑤

Ichiensō

Mankind exists in harmony with the universe. In bushidō one pursues the ideal of beauty at the moment of death. By practicing ichiensō, we strive to give a physical representation of the form of the universe, using our own body. When performing ichiensō, just after finishing reishiki and before starting our actual training, we visualize ourselves as one element of that universe. Needless to say, we cannot know the complexities of the universe, such as when it began and when it will end. Human beings know when they were born, but they do not know when they will die. Death may occur tomorrow, in ten years, in twenty years, or even in fifty years. From the moment one is born, one is destined to die; nobody has eternal life.

The most important mental attitude in bushidō is being prepared to die at any time. When conducting ichiensō, we not only prepare for our sword practice, but also for immediate death. Humans naturally harbor a primal fear of death, so we must begin by overcoming that fear. This is the very starting point of the study of bushidō, and of martial arts. Samurai must know about death first, and only later can they begin to understand the world.

①

②

③

SHODEN
(BEGINNING LEVEL)

Shoden is the first level of traditional sword technique. By the Edo period, when bushidō had evolved to the form recognized today, bushi and commoners alike would sit when indoors in seiza (formal sitting position) on traditional tatami mats. This meant that many iai techniques starting from the seiza position were developed. The purpose of shoden is to learn how to use the sword, starting from taitō (the position of the sword in the obi; see page 83), drawing the sword from its scabbard, slashing, thrusting, cutting, and finally how to return the sword back to the scabbard. Without following the correct procedure, the student might cause him or herself injury—before learning how to cut your opponent, you must learn not to cut yourself. In Enshin Ryū, shoden is also the foundation for iaijutsu and kenjutsu. It should be practiced with a sincere and pure mind.

Jūmonji ("no enemy"—the base of all iai kenpō kata)
Enshin Ryū's iai kenpō officially has forty-two kata. For each of these forty-two kata there are eighteen henka (variations), making a total of 756 different techniques. These henka contain many traditional fighting skills. Jūmonji is the base of all iai kenpō kata. These kata also include the idea of invoking divine protection, much like the ancient purification rites in shrines all over Japan, not only against external danger but also against evil spirits deep within one's mind. The characters used for jūmonji are 十文字: the first character depicts horizontal and vertical cuts which symbolize the purification of the soul.

After understanding the purification rite, students must learn the mental discipline of not willingly initiating com-

④

⑤

⑥

⑦

bat. Behind all kata is a spirit of peace—one should not make enemies and one does not willingly seek out an enemy. In jūmonji, the warrior can see and perceive all things with precision and clarity, as if viewing a landscape under a shining sun or a bright moon. In a wider perspective, this means that people in a position of responsibility, such as teachers or managers, should follow the purity of jūmonji, and their subordinates will in turn do the same, thus finding peace and prosperity. Accordingly, students of the sword—the soul of the samurai—should have no rivals, should cultivate peaceful thoughts, and should never seek out enemies.

In the application of this kata, the student learns the basics of sword drawing and sheathing. Hold the scabbard in the left hand and push the hilt of the sword away with the thumb ①–③. Holding the hilt in the right hand, and keeping it stationary, slide the scabbard back about 30 cm, then draw the sword clear of the scabbard with the right hand ④–⑤, extending both arms away from the body ⑥. Next, bring the miné (blunt edge) of the sword to the palm of the left hand ⑦ and raise the sword above the head with the left hand still resting on the miné ⑧. Bring the left hand to the hilt

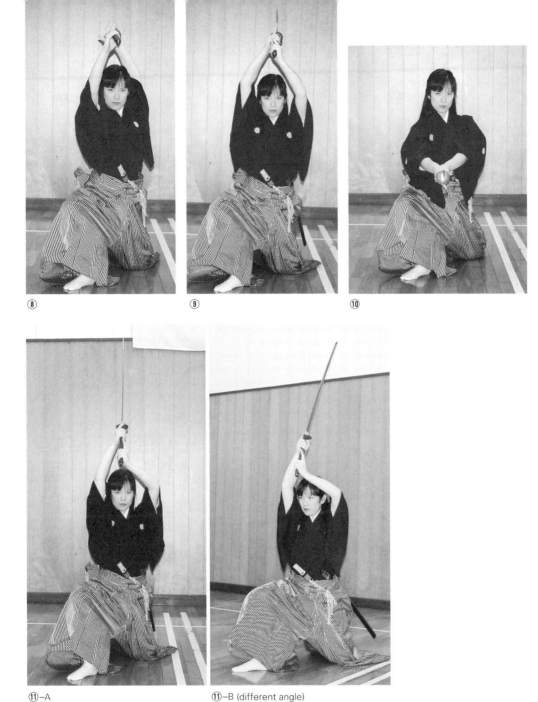

⑧   ⑨   ⑩

⑪–A   ⑪–B (different angle)

of the sword and make a makkō-uchi (frontal strike) ⑨–⑩. Next, assume jōdan-no-kamae ⑪ A+B, and, reversing the grip of the right hand, turn the sword away from the body to the right ⑫–⑬. The sword will be perpendicular to the body, representing the cross shape of the jū (十) character.

Sheathing the sword is of the utmost importance. First, drop the left hand, then bring the sword down so that the blunt edge can be gripped between the thumb and forefinger of the left hand ⑭–⑯. Place the tip of the sword in the scabbard and, keeping the right hand stationary, move the scabbard back over the blade with the left hand ⑰–⑳.

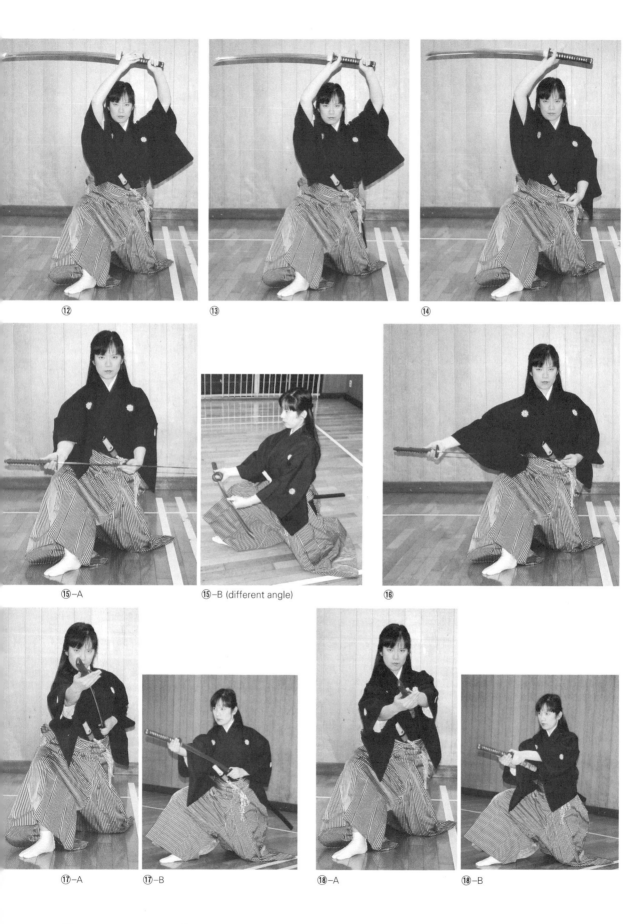

⑫

⑬

⑭

⑮-A

⑮-B (different angle)

⑯

⑰-A

⑰-B

⑱-A

⑱-B

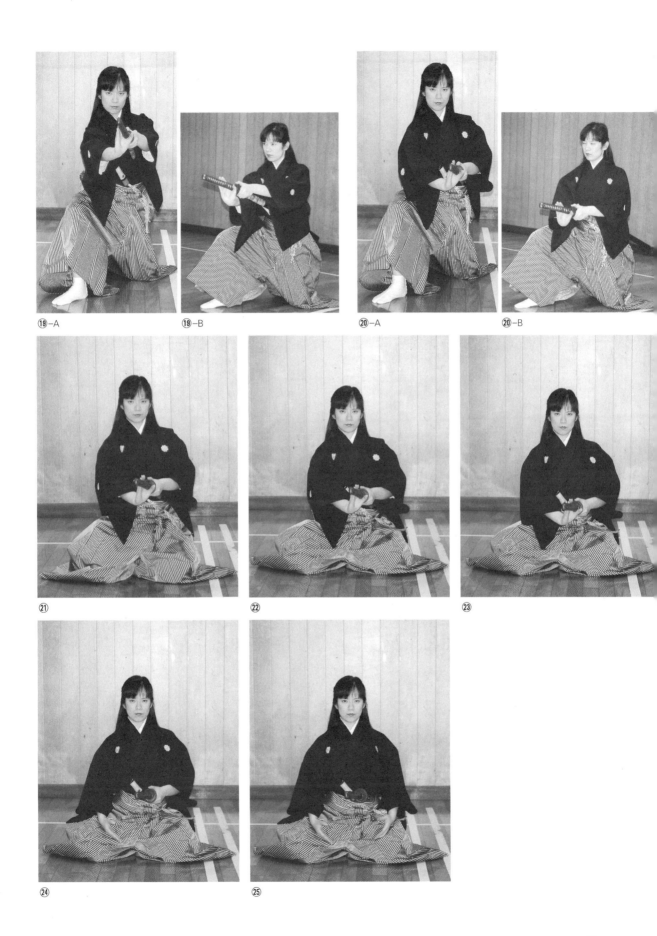

⑲-A ⑲-B ⑳-A ⑳-B

㉑ ㉒ ㉓

㉔ ㉕

① ② ③

④ ⑤

⑥

Jōiuchi ("the duty of loyalty")

After studying jūmonji and its philosophy, students must accept that it is forbidden to engage in fights for personal reasons. However, samurai were sometimes ordered by their lord to cut down an enemy or a criminal: the term "jōiuchi" means "to kill on higher orders." Just as modern-day soldiers must follow the orders of their superiors, a samurai had to obey the orders of his lord.

⑦ ⑧ ⑨

The judges watching jōiuchi being performed would have worn kamishimo (formal wear).

⑩

⑪-A ⑪-B (supplementary step) ⑪-C

This kata assumes an opponent is attacking from the right. Unsheathe the sword and extend the right arm to prevent the attacker from advancing further ①–⑥. Next, conduct a migi-kesauchi (right strike to the opponent's neck) ⑦–⑨. Quickly assume waki-gamae (guard position with the sword to one's side to conceal the arm) ⑩–⑪ B, and then raise the miné ⑫ to protect from possible further attacks from the enemy or an attack from behind. Should no more attacks occur, sheathe the sword following the same technique as that of jūmonji ⑱–㉕.

⑫ ⑬ ⑭

⑮ ⑯ ⑰

When judges watched jōiuchi being performed indoors from outside, they wore kamishimo as well as jingasa. There could watch either standing (left) or sitting on a stool (right).

⑱ ⑲ ⑳ ㉑ ㉒ ㉓ ㉔ ㉕

① ② ③
④ ⑤ ⑥

Jinrai ("samurai morals")

Even without intentionally seeking out enemies, a samurai could sometimes find himself under a surprise attack, or his sense of justice might have forced them to fight: in this case he had to deal with the situation immediately. Jinrai means that one should be ready to fight, whenever and wherever necessary. Samurai also had to be prepared to act as kaishaku, to assist a fellow samurai committing seppuku. Seppuku was considered the most important ritual in bushidō.

This kata begins with a left attack to the opponent's legs or shins. Draw the sword and make a low cut to prevent the opponent's attack ①–③. Raise the sword and perform a hidari-kesagiri (left diagonal cut from the opponent's neck to the waist) ④–⑥. Reverse the grip of the right hand and sheath the sword ⑦–⑬.

⑦   ⑧

⑨   ⑩

⑪   ⑫   ⑬

① ②

③ ④

Tendō ("the law of the universe")

In the war-ridden days of the Sengoku period, a warrior's main purpose was to survive on the battlefield, to be successful in combat, and to win promotion. Warriors who killed as many enemies on the battlefield as possible in order to raise their status were praised as heroes. This kind of ambition was called shogun gaku—"study to become shogun"—and was pursued by some of Japan's most important historical leaders, including Minamoto no Yoritomo (1147–1199), Ashikaga Takauji (1305–1358), Toyotomi Hideyoshi (1537–1598), and Tokugawa Ieyasu (1543–1616), founder of the Tokugawa shogunate. These men shared a common goal of advancement.

In times of peace, however, killing without just cause, or simply for social advancement, is never allowed. During the extended peace of the Edo period, the warriors of the previous period came to be regarded with some disdain, and many thought that they had abused their courage and brought great suffering to others.

⑤   ⑥

Without the correct mental framework, training students in the martial arts could be seen as nothing more than training people in violence. Practical training must be balanced with theoretical study and spiritual development. This is what is meant by bun-bu-ryōdō—the philosophy that considered literature and martial arts to be equally important.

The complexity of life demands a strong mind and character, which we can develop through martial arts training. The martial arts practitioner must also study a wide range of philosophies and academic pursuits, which help to develop a deeper understanding of life. These areas include: tendō ("the law of the universe"); chidō ("the law of earth"); jindō ("the law of mankind"); Shinto; and Buddhism, as well as astrology, geography, current events, chemistry, or natural science. Developing a strong body, and strong willpower, has beneficial ramifications for all kinds of spheres, whether politics, economics, culture, or the arts. This process is called teiōgaku—"study of the emperor."

The iai kata of tendō teaches students these values. This kata assumes an opponent is attacking from behind. Draw the sword and fully extend the right arm so the end of the sword is above head level ①–④. Turn round and perform a makkō-uchi ⑤–⑥ then quickly assume torii-gamae (upper guard position; the shape resembles the gate of a Shinto shrine) ⑦–⑧ A+B to prepare for any further attacks. End the kata by sheathing the sword and turning back around to assume the original position ⑨–⑳.

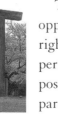

The torii of Ise Shrine.

⑦

Torii-gamae is assumed as a means of purifying the soul and spirit. The waterfall traditionally symbolizes divine nature; it is also thought to be a place visited and purified by dragons. Samurai sometimes assumed torii-gamae in front of waterfalls.

⑧-A

⑧-B (different angle)

⑨

⑩

⑪

① ② ③ ④

Aun ("the law of life and death")

This technique assumes a sudden attack from behind by an unknown enemy, in which death seems inevitable. The technique essentially teaches students that life and death are one. Using this technique, there is a strong possibility of death, but it ensures the enemy will die also. This is the essence of aiuchi ("mutual slaying").

The meaning of the term aun needs some explanation. When a child is born, the sound that accompanies his first inhalation is "ah." When he dies as an old man, the sound accompanying his last exhalation is "un." In Buddhism, this duality is known as "aun" and is based on a principle of completion and

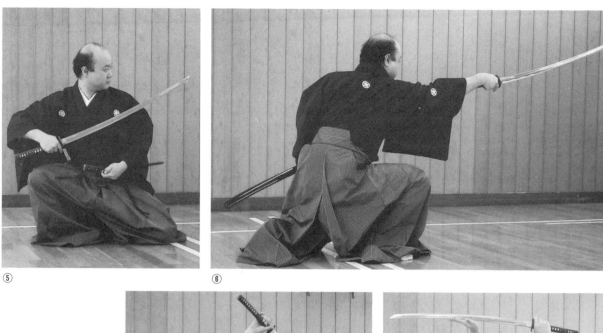

⑤   ⑥

⑦   ⑧

mutual understanding, and of bringing together opposite concepts. Similarly, when faced with a sudden sword attack, it is necessary to draw the sword and understand the enemy's mind immediately in readiness for death, both for oneself and one's enemy.

For this kata, draw the sword, turn around and perform a tsuki (thrust) ①–⑥. To deal a fatal blow to the enemy if they are still alive, and to defend from further attacks from behind, assume shimei-gamae ("fatal-blow position") ⑦. Finish the kata by sheathing the sword and returning to the original position ⑧–㉑.

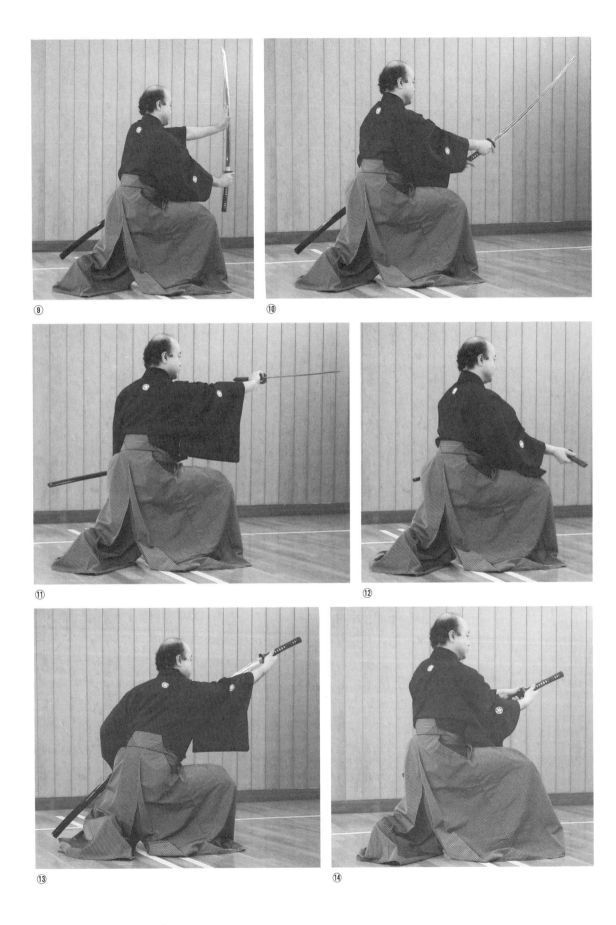

⑮

⑯

One of the Deva kings (guardian gods of a temple gate), posing in "ah."

Another Deva king posing in "un."

⑰

⑱

⑲

⑳

㉑

① ② ③ ④

Mujin ("killing enemies in six directions")

Social situations constantly change, and conflicts between individuals frequently arise. If one is faced with the situation of having to kill an enemy, one should assume there could be more than just one enemy. The purpose of this technique is to master footwork, body movement, and sword manipulation to survive by killing multiple enemies one after another. In this kata, the student learns how to fight enemies coming from six directions, so this technique is sometimes also called rokusatsu-ken (literally, "six-killing sword").

As in the kata of aun, draw the sword, turn, and perform a tsuki ①–⑤. Pull the sword back, and conduct a second tsuki ⑥–⑧. Next, conduct a migi-kesagiri (right diagonal cut from the opponent's neck to the waist) ⑨–⑩, then extend the sword in the direction of another enemy to prevent them advancing ⑪. At this point begin sheathing the sword ⑫–⑱, but should any more enemies attack, perform additional tsuki.

⑤

⑥

⑦

⑧

⑨

⑩

⑪

⑫

⑬

⑭

⑮

⑯

⑰

⑱

Sassō ("the way of feeling and seeing")

In kenjutsu and iaijutsu, it is important to gain an insight into an enemy's movements and intentions. There are two ways of "looking" at an opponent—kan (feeling), and ken (seeing). Kan is like a mental overview, sensing the opponent's intentions: seeing, as it were, with one's heart. Ken is seeing the actual situation with one's eyes. The sassō kata prepares the student's mind to sense the enemy's sakki ("killing intention") as quickly as possible.

Enshin Ryū teaches how to defend oneself from an unseen enemy from behind. In order to sense what cannot be seen, it is important to develop the sixth sense, a state of subconscious awareness. Enshin Ryū goes beyond this, however, and teaches students how to develop no less than nine senses.

We have five senses—sight, hearing, smell, taste, and touch—that enable us to perceive the substance of something tangible. An invisible substance, or an unseen enemy, is perceived through the sixth sense (rokkan or roku shiki). In Enshin Ryū, students must develop their inner consciousness to a much profounder degree: through the seventh sense, called manashiki; the eighth sense, arayashiki; to the ninth sense, kushiki shinnō. Kushiki is the unfettered mind, the most sublime state of consciousness attainable: it is the state in which one comprehends the substance and essence of everything.

In martial arts, as well as in society, opponents or enemies, and the situations in which they can appear, are often unknown. Despite this one should never be puzzled about what to do when encountering an opponent, or about the opponent's conduct or intentions. One should also have no fear that the opponent may be stronger, have better skills and more weapons, or more supporters. This is the essence of fudōshin, or the unmovable heart. After having acquired perfect fudōshin through training and study, it is possible to say one has developed the ninth sense.

This kata trains students to sense an unseen attack. The example shown here assumes an attacker who has grabbed the swordsman's clothing from behind to pull him down. Slide the left leg forward and circle round on the knee while at the same time drawing the sword ①–⑤. When circling, transfer onto the left knee and raise the right knee. Perform a tsuki ⑥, then a migi-kesauchi ⑦–⑨. Keeping the shoulders relaxed, rise, holding the sword in suishin-gamae (downward position, as if holding a fishing line straight into a pool) ⑩. Once standing, raise the sword over the head with the right arm, then bring it down in a half circle to the right ⑪–⑬. End the kata by sheathing the sword ⑭–⑳.

① ② ③ ④ ⑤ ⑥

⑦

⑧

⑨

⑩

The posture suishin-gamae in the photo ⑩ expresses restraint of emotions even after killing an opponent. The scene of the Nō drama *Kanawa* also expresses the restraint of emotions, especially spite.

⑪

⑫

⑬

⑭-A ⑭-B

⑮ ⑯ ⑰

⑱ ⑲ ⑳

Migi santen ("killing an enemy to the right")

This kata teaches how to deal quickly with an opponent coming from the right-hand side, or how to chase an opponent to the right-hand side and cut him. Students learn the combat skill of entering into what the opponent perceives as his personal safety zone, thus limiting his room for maneuver.

① ② ③ ④ ⑤ ⑥ ⑦ ⑧ ⑨

Naka santen ("protecting the head")

This kata teaches how to use tachisabaki (sword manipulation) against an enemy directly in front. The sword is used to cover the head in a position that will enable the student to attack while also providing protection for the head in the event of an attack from behind (note the position in pictures ⑤, ⑨, ⑬, and ⑰). This kata therefore unifies attack and defense.

①

②

Hidari santen ("the way of water")

This form is sometimes known as "the method of square and circle." In Enshin Ryū, kata are compared to water. Water is formless, and can assume any shape—if water is put into a square vessel, it will take on that shape; if put into a round vessel, it will take on a round shape.

Likewise, when using a sword, the swordsman must keep in mind this essence of mutability and the idea of square and circle. The swordsman must become like water; without shape and without thoughts. Just as water is free to flow, the swordsman should not limit his fighting style, and must keep a calm mind. The calm mind, uncluttered by thoughts, is called mushin.

Hidari santen is the reverse of migi santen—the enemy is chased to the left and cut down. Executing this kata straight to the left is known as hō-no-kata (the square form) ①–⑥. If the opponent avoids the cut, however, and moves behind (to the left), it is necessary to turn toward the opponent and kill him with a diagonal downward cut. This form is known as en-no-kata (the circular form) ⑦–⑩.

These three kata—hidari santen, migi santen and naka santen—teach two very important principles of sword technique and footwork: first, how to drive your opponent in a certain direction and, second, how to remain in a central position and cut the enemy down while pivoting around your own body.

③

④

⑤

⑥

⑦

⑧

⑨ ⑩

⑪ ⑫

⑬ ⑭

⑮ ⑯ ⑰ ⑱ ⑲ ⑳

① ② ③ ④

Hakuryū ("white dragon")

The techniques from the first kata, jūmonji, through to the tenth, hidari santen, are all for indoor use, and all start from seiza. From hakuryū onward, techniques start either from walking, or from a standing position. Hakuryū is the standing version of naka santen. Essential principles to be learned include ashisabaki (footwork), the degree of bending one's knees, the height of the waist, and the balance of the upper body. While engaged in combat, one has to maintain good stability, use correct rhythm, and keep the timing of kōbō ittai—the principle that attack and defense are executed simultaneously.

Hakuryū means "white dragon." The white dragon is seen as the heavenly messenger. In ancient times, there was a saying: "Defeat evil by personifying heaven." Similarly, in bushidō, the student learns the mental attitude to destroy evil, using justice to defeat his enemies.

Through the practice of iai kenpō, the student can educate himself to become an extraordinary person, possessing intelligence, culture, a good character, and strong social skills. The individual who has a sound capacity to evaluate any situation, whether private or social, and determine right from wrong, is revered as the dragon.

⑤ ⑥ ⑦

⑧ ⑨ ⑩

The kata begins from a standing position, and assumes an opponent is attacking from the front. Draw the sword quickly, raise it above the head, and perform a makkō-uchi ①–⑦. Next, raise the sword, tilting the blade to the left perpendicular to the body—this posture enables both attack and defense—⑧, and perform another makkō-uchi ⑨–⑩. Repeat this process tilting the sword to the right ⑪–⑬, and then one further time to the left ⑭–⑯. Assume kensei-no-kamae (sword extended forward to prevent enemies advancing) ⑰ for two or three seconds, then sheath the sword ⑱–㉓.

⑪ ⑫ ⑬

⑭ ⑮ ⑯

Hakuryū. In Japan fountains at temples or shrines are sometimes made in the shape of dragons and the water flowing from their mouths is called ryūsui ("dragon water"). Before praying, people rinse out their mouths and wash their hands in this water.

⑰ ⑱ ⑲ ⑳

㉑ ㉒ ㉓

①   ②

Inazuma ("flash of lightning")

The inazuma kata is the simplest one to learn; nevertheless, the simpler the kata, the more difficult it becomes when used in a real situation. In this kata, the student learns the principle of jo-ha-kyū. From ancient times, all performances of gagaku (imperial court music), bugaku (imperial court dance), Nōgaku (Nō theater) and kabuki (classical theater), were based on the three phases of jo-ha-kyū. This principle is central to all expressions of bujutsu, but in no technique is it more clearly expressed than in inazuma.

In Japan, from ancient mythological times, people saw all aspects of nature—including the sun, moon, and stars, the clouds, thunder, rivers, waterfalls, and waves—as acts performed by various gods, and throughout history they have worshipped these acts. In these acts, they have discerned three parts: a beginning, a middle, and an end, and these are called jo-ha-kyū.

Jo is the gradual action that occurs from stillness, such as starting to walk from a static position—beginning from nothing. Ha is the continuation of various acts deriving from jo; the movement of walking freely, for example. Kyū is the highest development of general ability, in which the walk develops into a run at full speed. Finally, one returns again to the static position, completing the cycle, which is repeated over and over. This is called kyakurai, or the law of rotation.

③

Samurai learned tenmon (astronomy) as part of hyōhō (steategy). This picture depicts inazuma from a scroll relating to astoronomy.

The principle of jo-ha-kyū can be applied to the cycle of human life. To begin, a child is born from the stasis of mu (the void). At first the movement of the infant is slow—this is the jo phase. As the child grows he begins to learn and gain knowledge, and this continues throughout his youth—the ha phase. In adulthood and middle age he is able to apply his abilities to a wider range of activities and with a higher degree of skill. This is the kyū phase; the peak of his abilities. After this period is finished, he becomes an old man, and begins to lose his physical and mental faculties. His moves are once again slow, as when he was a baby.

The inazuma kata teaches drawing the sword and returning it back to the scabbard using the jo-ha-kyū principle. First, starting from nothing (mu), grip the sword's scabbard with the left hand and hilt with the right, then break the seal of the sword by pushing the tsuba (sword-guard) with the thumb of the left hand, so that about 3 cm of the sword is out of the scabbard ①–②. This action is described in Japanese as koiguchi o kiru, and represents the jo phase. Next, keeping the right hand stationary, pull the scabbard toward the belt with the left hand ③. This is the ha phase. Finally, coordinating the right hand and the left side of the waist, quickly draw the sword from the scabbard ④–⑤. This is the kyū phase. Other actions and movements may still be conducted after this. Finally, return the sword back to the scabbard ⑥–⑪, so it is once again in the situation of nothingness (mu).

Inazuma means a "sudden flash of lightning." The sword must be drawn like lightning to cut the enemy down in an instant. Full mastery of this technique allows the practitioner to cut down an enemy even if the enemy has drawn his sword first.

⑧　⑨　⑩　⑪

① ② ③ ④

⑤ ⑥ ⑦

⑧ ⑨

Depiction of "purple lightning" from a scroll relating to astronomy.

Shiden ("purple lightning")

Shiden is the continuation of inazuma. This technique assumes that, after cutting down an opponent with the inazuma technique ①–⑧, another enemy suddenly attacks from behind while the sword is being sheathed ⑨. Once again draw the sword, and this time attack the enemy in aiuchi fashion ⑩–⑫. The key here is to swiftly draw the sword again while it is being sheathed.

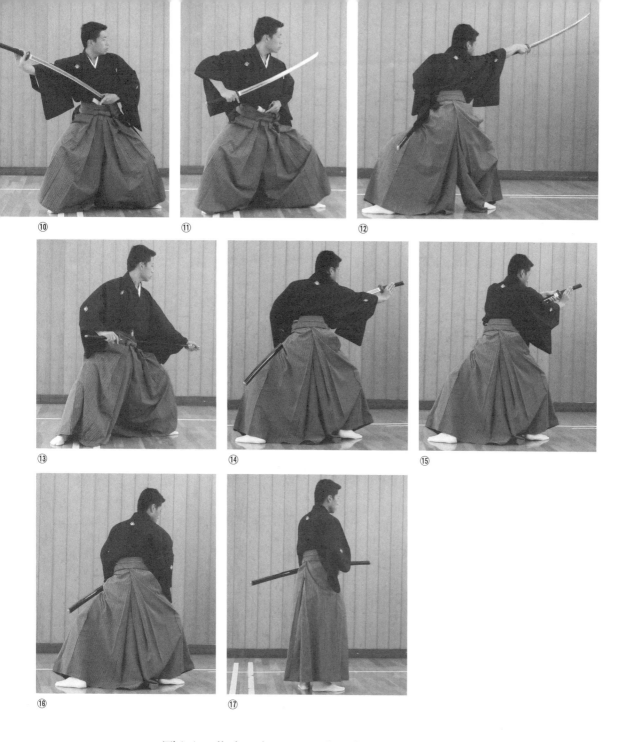

This is called nō-batsu-no-nihō; the method of drawing (battō) and sheathing (nōtō).

Shiden means "purple lightning," and is considered to be more distinguished than normal inazuma. The scabbard is seen as the clouds and the sword the lightning strike, as in the inazuma technique, but the extra value added to this lightning strike is its "purple light," or its majestic swiftness. In order to successfully accomplish this technique, the student has to develop the ability to draw the sword quickly to neutralize a surprise attack while conducting nōtō.

Depiction of "white lightning" from a scroll relating to astronomy. White lightning refers to the appearance of three lightning bolts at once, which makes the sky as light as day.

Hakuden ("white lightning" or "special breathing")

Hakuden teaches the principle of kokyū, or breathing, a special technique in Enshin Ryū. Controlled breathing is vital in combat. Without it, the enemy can take advantage of suki ("unguarded moments") that can be created by erratic breathing. This breathing method is called chūkan kokyū ("inhale half, exhale half"), and is designed to disguise the inhaling and exhaling movements of breathing from the enemy.

Unrai ("thunder from the clouds")

Although a swordsman might have strong fighting skills and generally perform well in combat, he might sometimes have to fight under difficult circumstances, and be prone to unexpected, potentially fatal mistakes. In this way, bushidō mirrors life—in difficult times it is natural that one has to make extra effort, taking advantage of one's general ability to overcome adversity.

In Enshin Ryū, the unrai kata teaches the mental framework necessary to fight under both good and bad circumstances. These circumstances are compared to wind, and it is possible to say that in good circumstances, the swordsman has the wind in his back. Conversely, in bad circumstances, he has to contend with a head wind. In Enshin Ryū, however, there is a saying: "There is neither a favorable nor an unfavorable wind." This means that we should be in command of our own abilities, and in this way, turn any adverse winds to our advantage. This is called gyaku-soku-ze-jun, or "turning unfavorable winds into favorable ones."

To perform this kata, use the right hand in gyakute ("reversed gripping") style. Through unrai, the student can master the reversed technique and use it to draw the sword, practice tachisabaki, and fight an opponent. Thus the student can gain the ability to fight using an orthodox or an unorthodox style.

CHŪDEN
(INTERMEDIATE LEVEL)

In shoden, students learn reigi, and iai kenpō techniques that mainly focus on indoor fighting situations starting from seiza. On reaching chūden, however, the student learns outdoor techniques for use on the battlefield.

Kenuken ("lightning sword")

In old times warriors needed to fight from horseback, because the outcome of a war largely depended on mobility. This kata teaches the basic technique for fighting from horseback. The idea behind the kata is that an enemy, also mounted on horseback, approaches from the right-hand side. Tighten the thighs and push the right heel into his horse's flank to turn the horse to the right ①–⑦. Next, draw the sword upward, and then slash down to the right with the right hand ⑧–⑬. This kata is designed for outdoor fighting.

①

②

③

④

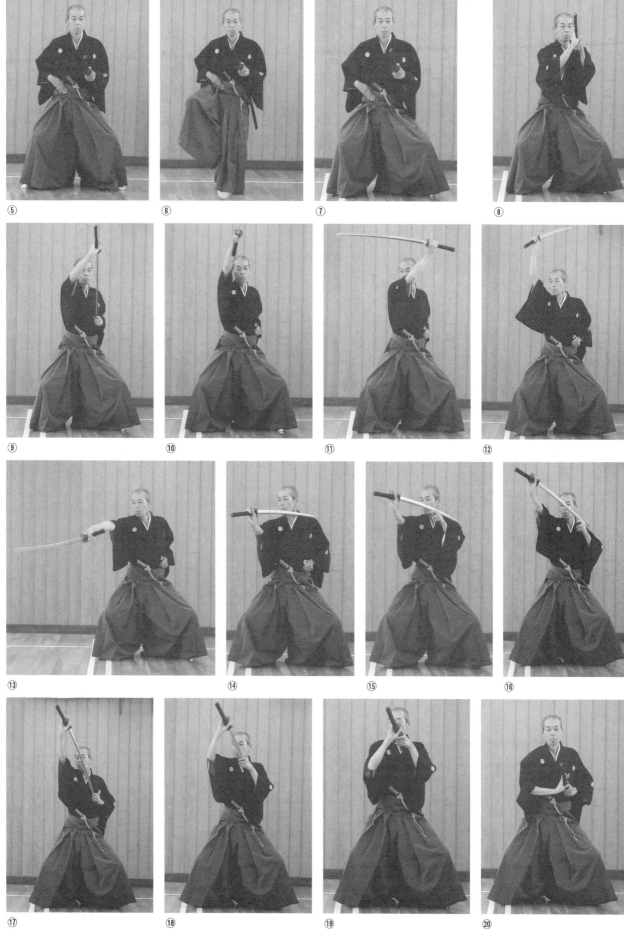

① ② ③

④ ⑤ ⑥

Kensaken ("thunder sword")

In this kata, the same principle as that of kenuken is used, but the intent is
to cut down an enemy approaching from the left—steering the horse to the
left, and kicking the left heel into the horse's left flank. It must be remem-
bered that from old days it has been taught that the warrior should see his
horse as a vital ally, and not simply as a means of transportation or a fighting
instrument. When training this technique in the dōjō (practice hall), the
student should adopt the same mentality as a mounted samurai.

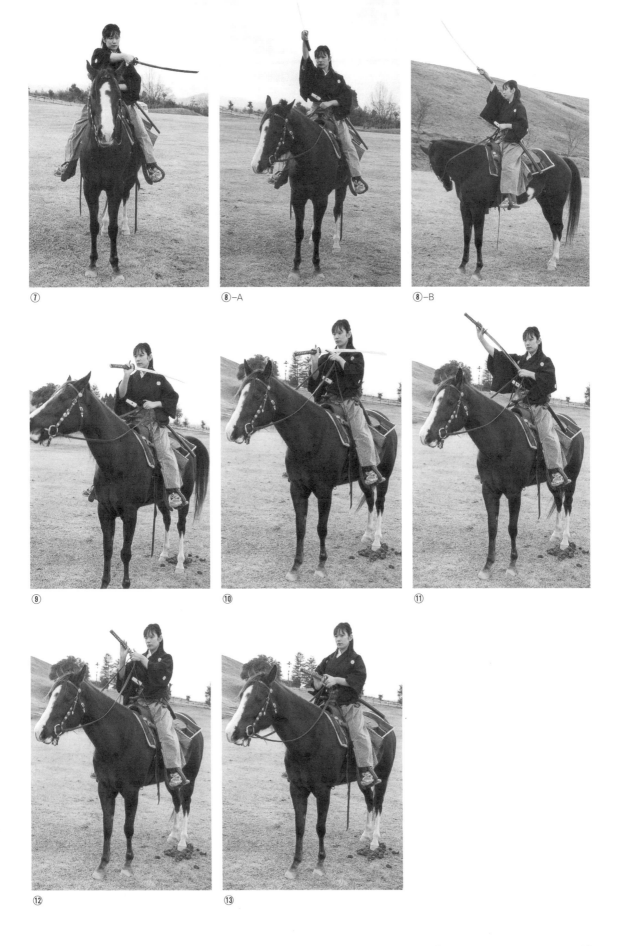

⑦   ⑧-A   ⑧-B

⑨   ⑩   ⑪

⑫   ⑬

① ② ③ ④ ⑤ ⑥ ⑦ ⑧ ⑨ ⑩ ⑪

Konuken ("right-circling sword")

This kata teaches how to break through a line of multiple enemies to the front. First, face one enemy and perform nukitsuke (fast drawing and cutting) or makkō-uchi (in this example, nukitsuke is used). Next, pursue the

⑫ ⑬ ⑭

⑮ ⑯ ⑰

⑱ ⑲ ⑳

enemy with a migi-kesauchi ⑥–⑦, in order to break through the line. It is possible to perform kesagiri (diagonal cut) after the nukitsuke—⑧–⑭—while turning around to the right using the right foot as a pivot. After having executed three cuts in this way, the swordsman will return to face the same direction as when he started. In this example, the swordsman has used both the kesauchi and kesagiri techniques.

Konsaken ("left-circling sword")

This is the left-side version of konuken. Pivot to the left using the left foot, while repeating diagonal cuts (kesauchi or kesagiri). The key lies in harmonious and rhythmical footwork and swordwork. Another name for konsaken and konuken is fūshaken, or "windmill sword," because of the way the movements resemble the rotation of a windmill.

① ② ③ ④

⑤ ⑥ ⑦ ⑧

Konchūken ("center-cut sword")

This kenpō technique is used when facing three opponents. First, cut down the opponent directly in front using a makkō-uchi ②–⑦. Next, cut down the opponent to the right with a migi kesagiri ⑧–⑩, then cut down the enemy to the left with a hidari kesagiri ⑪–⑬. In the furitsu ("no-rule") version of this technique, the practitioner is surrounded by four enemies. First, cut the enemy in front with a makkō-uchi, and then immediately turn around and cut the enemy behind, also using a makkō-uchi. Then, cut the enemy who at that time is to the left with a hidari kesagiri, and next the enemy who was originally to the right with a migi kesagiri. In this maneuver it is difficult for the enemies to spot an attack pattern, and this can be highly advantageous.

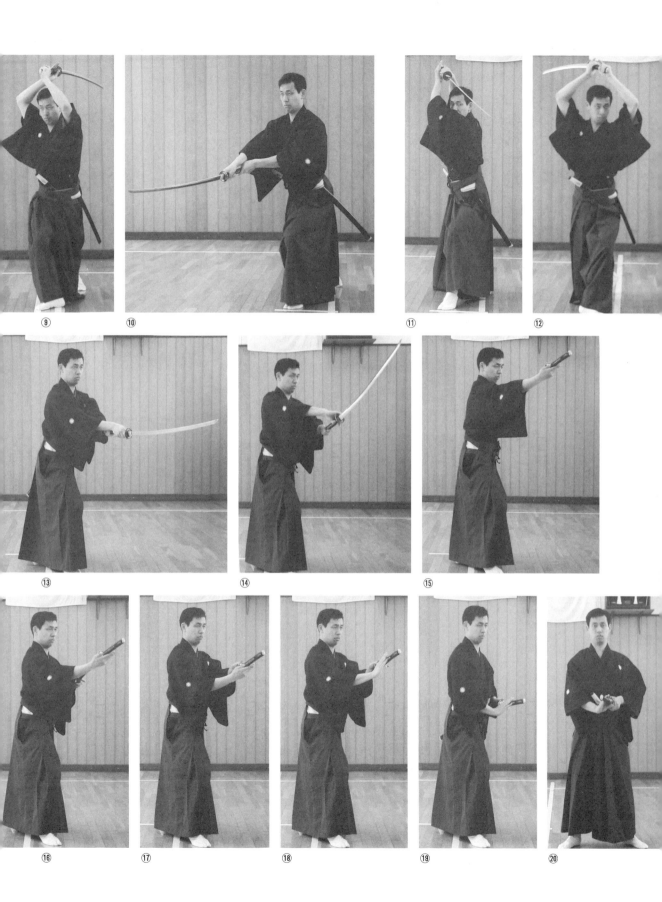

⑨ ⑩ ⑪ ⑫

⑬ ⑭ ⑮

⑯ ⑰ ⑱ ⑲ ⑳

Nō mask in the hannya style. The mind of a person plotting an assassination is full of the anger and jealousy seen on this mask.

① ② ③ ④ ⑤

Musōken ("no-thought sword")

Hayashizaki Jinsuke (1542–1617?) was a renowned samurai. He is known as the restorer of iaijutsu for his painstaking work to improve the sword-drawing techniques and to enhance already existing fighting techniques in iai. A story tells that one day, while he was out walking, he sensed sakki (intention to kill) coming from behind. He drew his sword and immediately made a horizontal cut behind his back, cutting the enemy in half. It is said that at that time Hayashizaki used his sword in munen musō fashion. This means that he was free from all thoughts. This kata is thus called musōken (literally, "no-thought sword").

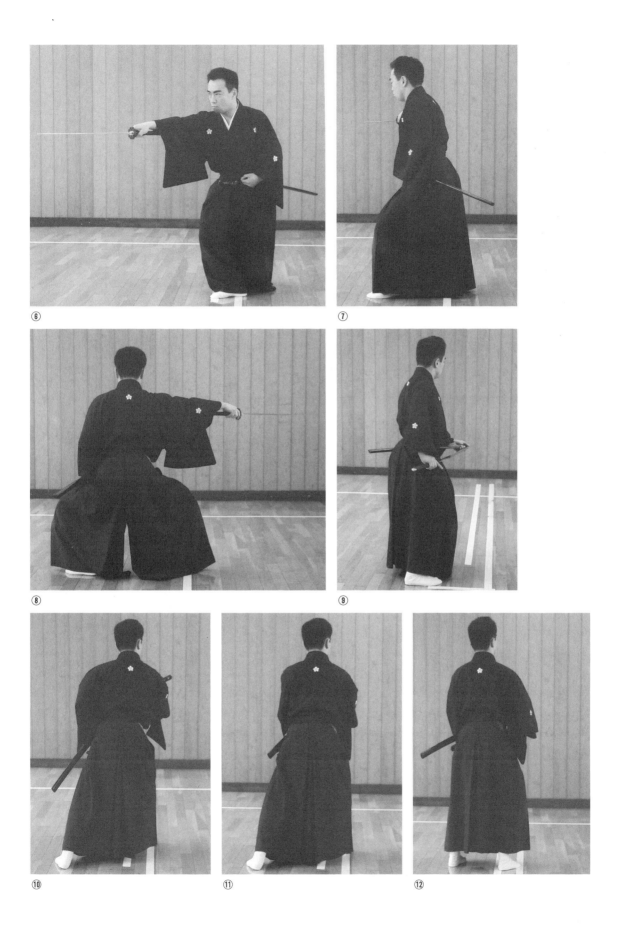

⑥ ⑦ ⑧ ⑨ ⑩ ⑪ ⑫

① ② ③

④ ⑤ ⑥

Hien ("jumping monkey")

The name of this kata, which is translated as "jumping monkey," relates to an old story, *Danchō no Omoi* ("Broken Heart"). According to the story, a hunter once caught a baby monkey, and took it down the river on his boat. It is said that when it comes to the love of a mother for her child, there is no difference between a human and an animal. The mother monkey thus tried desperately to rescue her baby. She jumped onto a rock that was in the river, and then onto another, and another, and finally, with one big leap, she jumped into the hunter's boat. No sooner had she entered the boat, however, than she suddenly died. Puzzled by this mysterious death, the hunter cut open the mother's belly and found her intestines were ripped apart—caused, he was later to assume, by her love for her child. In her sheer desire to get the child back, she had used too much power and energy.

⑦ ⑧ ⑨

⑩ ⑪ ⑫ ⑬

Some elements in the kata of hien are similar to the story. First, draw the sword and thrust to the rear, to stop any enemies that might have come from behind (this stage is omitted in the example shown here). Next, cut horizontally to chase an enemy away, and repeat this two more times ①–⑧. Though the swordwork should not change, the footwork should vary depending on where the kata is being executed. For example, chasing an enemy toward a wall involves making three horizontal cuts, and keeping one's feet firmly on the ground. Against an enemy who is moving away on stepping-stones in a river or pond, however, the swordsman must lift his right leg and, like the mother monkey from the story, jump to the next stepping-stone, while making a horizontal cut. It is possible also to thrust at the enemy with one hand. Jumping onto stepping-stones from some distance requires great power from stomach and waist, as it did for the mother monkey. This kata appears easy to learn, but its application in various situations demands considerable skill.

Hachiryūken ("eight-dragons sword")

From this stage on, the student learns not only martial arts fighting skills but also the concept of how a man of outstanding ability should behave. According to *Ekikyō* ("the I-Ching Book of Changes") a man of outstanding ability is called a "dragon," and this name is also used to refer to an intelligent, cultivated swordsman.

The hachiryūken series includes eight iai kenpō kata that are closely related and named after eight different dragons. The eight techniques deal with situations that could occur after the swordsman falls from his horse in combat, or after being thrown or kicked down by an enemy. In order to survive the swordsman needs sound kumiuchi and jūjutsu skills.

In addition to the practical techniques, the student needs to learn the deeper meaning and philosophy that is associated with each individual dragon, in order to develop his ability. The student of these techniques should also keep in mind that, just as in combat he might have enemies attacking from behind, it is necessary to be prepared to deal with similar situations in normal society.

■ ■ ■

SENRYŪ ("HIDDEN DRAGON" OR "SUBMERGED DRAGON")

Each individual has a certain special talent. If one wants to become an extraordinary person, however, then one needs to recognize this inherent, natural talent and improve it.

Someone who has the potential to become a "dragon" may still be presented with an array of obstacles. For instance, he may not yet have recognized his talent, or he could be uncertain as to how to proceed with it. He might lack experience, or might not yet have been discovered by those around him. In these cases, he cannot be called a "dragon." He is, as it were, a "hidden dragon," or a "submerged dragon." Perhaps society has no need for him yet, and he needs to stay out of sight, waiting for his time to come. Despite this, he should continue to develop his skills, so that when he is called upon to exercise his talent, he will be able to use it successfully.

The main idea behind the application of this kata (shown at right) is to use something as a shield. A warrior who, despite his talent, lacks real combat experience, or is uncertain about the skill of his opponent, might be wise to take advantage of any objects around him and use them as a shield. If suddenly attacked from behind by an enemy when walking, for example, the swordsman might instantly run and seek cover under a ledge, or run out of sight, or hide in the shade of trees and shrubs; essentially, make use of his surroundings to avoid attack while at the same time drawing his sword to fight the enemy.

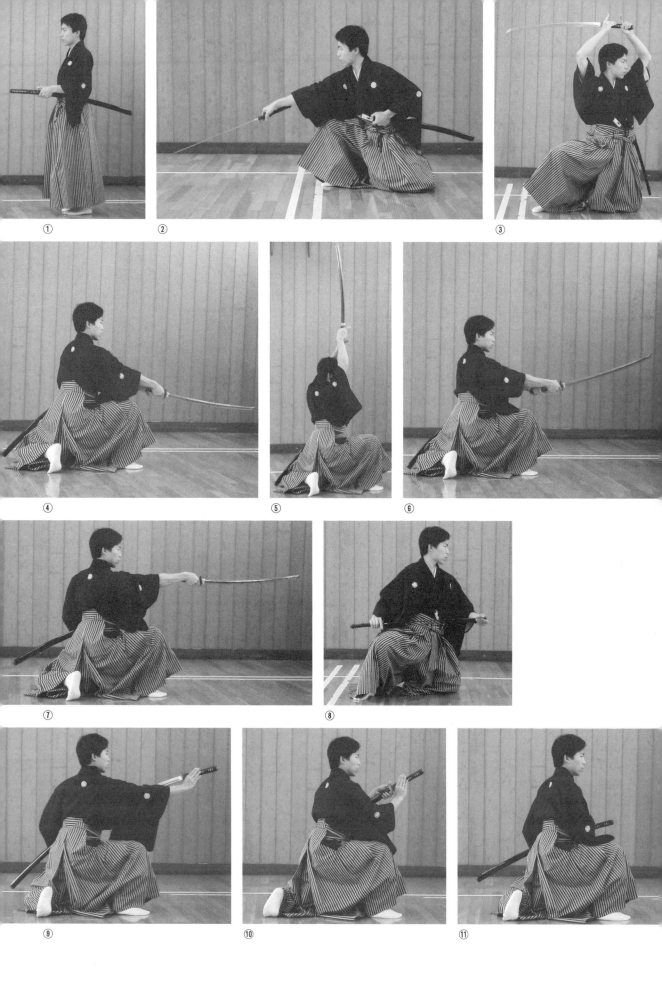

①　　　　　　　　　②　　　　　　　　　③

④　　　　　　　　　⑤　　　　　　　　　⑥

⑦　　　　　　　　　⑧

⑨　　　　　　　　　⑩　　　　　　　　　⑪

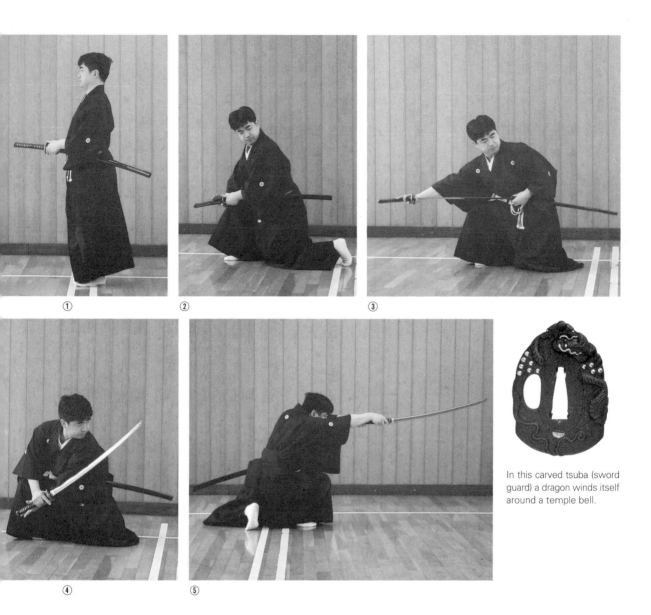

① ② ③

④ ⑤

In this carved tsuba (sword guard) a dragon winds itself around a temple bell.

CHIRYŪ ("DRAGON IN A POND")

A man can be called a "dragon" only when his talent is acknowledged by others. There is, however, what is known as a "dragon in the pond." This is a person who is modest, patient, and discreet. He waits calmly for the right time to act, like a dragon swimming in a pond; sometimes diving, sometimes surfacing, until circumstances finally allow him to exercise his talent in society.

The kata itself assumes that an enemy strikes the swordsman from behind while he is walking, or an enemy kicks him down while they are both engaged in a sword fight. Using the ukemi (breakfall) technique of jūjutsu, drop down on one knee ①–②, draw the sword ③–④, and thrust at the enemy ⑤. In iai practice, the ukemi is usually omitted.

① ② ③

④ ⑤ ⑥

⑦ ⑧ ⑨

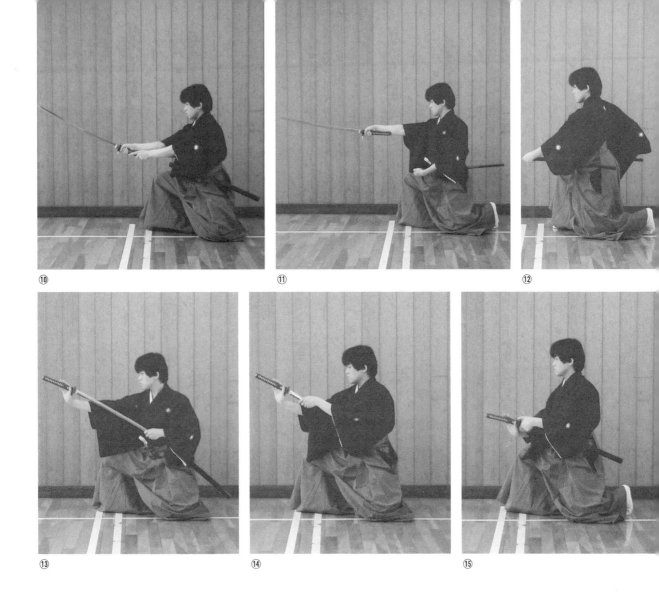

⑩　　　　　⑪　　　　　⑫

⑬　　　　　⑭　　　　　⑮

DENRYŪ ("DRAGON IN A RICE FIELD")

One meaning of denryū refers to the phase in a man's personal growth in which he becomes able to make use of his ability as a "dragon," and assume an active, influential role in society. If he is also noticed by his superiors or people of a higher social status, then it is possible to increase his status. The denryū, therefore, is similar to chiryū, and means "waiting for one's chance."

The kata is also similar to that of chiryū. An enemy suddenly attacks from behind. In the formal version of this technique, apply jūjutsu's ukemi and assume a low position kneeling on the left knee. Alternatively, simply drop down and take a low position on one knee ①–③, and then draw the sword from the scabbard to continue the fight.

① ② ③ ④

⑤ ⑥

UNRYŪ ("DRAGON IN THE CLOUDS")

According to an old proverb, "A dragon summons a cloud, a tiger invites the wind." The dragon and tiger have traditionally represented something or someone wielding great power and importance. In the Sengoku, or Warring States, period, for example, the great warlord Uesugi Kenshin (1530–78) was called a dragon, and his rival, Takeda Shingen, was called a tiger. They engaged in battle several times at Kawanakajima, and their battles were perceived as fights to the death between a dragon and tiger. Unryū refers to the phase when a man of special ability applies his talent, and becomes successful. It is natural that once he achieves notable success at a high level, regardless of his specialty or field, rivalries and jealousies will emerge, leading to a host of potential conflicts. These kinds of situation are compared to the clouds, the wind, or a storm.

The unryū iai kata assumes that the swordsman is surrounded by enemies and is suddenly attacked. As in senryū and chiryū, drop down on one knee to reduce the effect of the enemy's attack, and quickly draw the sword to thrust at the enemy who is directly behind ①–⑤. Then, cut down the enemy to the right using a migi kesauchi ⑥–⑧.

Drawing of unryū.

⑦　　　　　　⑧　　　　　　⑨

⑩　　　　　　⑪　　　　　　⑫　　　　　　⑬

⑭　　　　　　⑮　　　　　　⑯

A carved tsuba depicting a tenryū.

① ② ③ ④ ⑤ ⑥

TENRYŪ ("DRAGON IN THE SKY")

After having overcome conflict and rivalry, a man is finally respected as a leader who has asserted mastery of his field, whatever it may be. He has also reached an elevated social position. This stage is called tenryū.

In the iai kata, as in unryū, it is assumed that the swordsman is surrounded and attacked by several enemies. Kneel on one knee and draw the sword ①–④. Turn, and thrust behind ⑤–⑥, and make a chain of three continuous migi kesauchi to the right to break the attack ⑦–⑫, based on the taisabaki and tachisabaki of senryū, chiryū, and denryū.

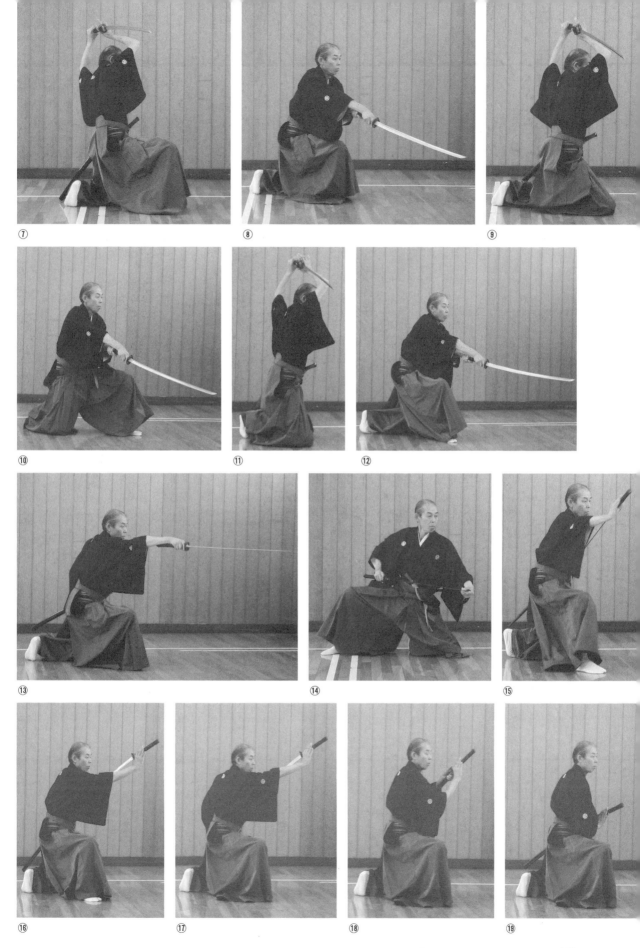

⑦ ⑧ ⑨ ⑩ ⑪ ⑫ ⑬ ⑭ ⑮ ⑯ ⑰ ⑱ ⑲

① ② ③

④ ⑤

⑥

A tsuba inlaid with two hiryū.

HIRYŪ ("FLYING DRAGON")

After mastering the tenryū stage, a man of special ability generates one success after another. He is supported by his superiors and other influential people. In this phase, he is known as hiryū, or "flying dragon."

The iai kata is similar to that of unryū, but in this case it is necessary to perform a hidari kesauchi (left strike to the opponent's neck), as the enemy is approaching from the left-hand side.

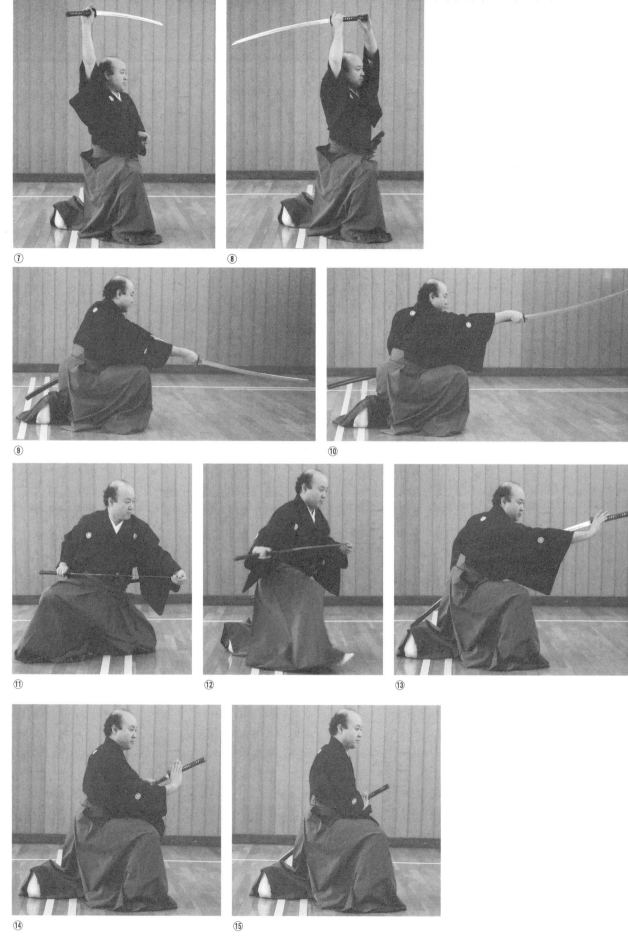

⑦ ⑧

⑨ ⑩

⑪ ⑫ ⑬

⑭ ⑮

① ② ③ ④

⑤ ⑥ ⑦

KŌRYŪ ("EXCITED DRAGON")

In this stage, the "dragon" has grown so strong that he can now succeed in every activity to the point of feeling invincible. Nevertheless, if he becomes too arrogant and loses humility, he is likely to suffer a loss of popularity and fall into misfortune. Applied to the business world this could mean, for example, bankruptcy, or it is possible that one becomes disliked and even betrayed by close friends. In the stage of kōryū, therefore, one has to remain careful so as not, so to speak, to fall from the sky.

The tachisabaki of kōryū is the reverse of that of tenryū—for this kata perform three continuous hidari kesauchi.

GUNRYŪ ("A MULTITUDE OF DRAGONS")

Gunryū represents the final stage in the growth of the "dragon." A man has reached perfect ability through his constant efforts and has advanced from senryū to kōryū, but, crucially, he never forgets humility and progresses very steadily. In *Ekikyō*, it is said that "gunryū has many faces." This means a man's ability is so great and diverse, and he has achieved such worthiness, that he has attained near-perfection. A man is called gunryū, for example, when he has become versed in every aspect of the martial arts, but is also a scholar of great knowledge, and has built up a network of connections, reaching all levels of society.

⑪　⑫　⑬
⑭　⑮　⑯
⑰　⑱　⑲　⑳

In iai, from senryū to kōryū, the student studies techniques starting from a kneeling position on one knee. In gunryū, the student learns the technique of standing up from the kneeling position, running forward toward the enemy, and cutting him. In this technique, a special form of ashisabaki (footwork) known as kobashiri—a way of running using very small steps—is used. Considerable practice is therefore essential. In Enshin Ryū's iai kenpō, the tsuki is considered the ultimate technique. In the gunryū kata, surrounded by enemies, the student learns how to run and thrust back and forth, both to his right and left. The kobashiri in this technique is illustrated in pictures ⑦– ⑪, and, using this, the student has to master the ability to break an attack from any direction. The kata expresses figuratively how a grown dragon moves.

① ② ③

④ ⑤ ⑥ ⑦

Jōiuchi ("execution order")

Enshin Ryū students study the basic pattern of jōiuchi in the shoden stage. In the chūden level the student is taught the practical kata that was used in real situations.

Jōiuchi was an execution order from a feudal lord. If a man of samurai rank was found guilty of malpractice, or committed a serious crime such as murder, robbery, or arson, it was the common practice for his lord to order him to conduct seppuku. If, however, he didn't obey or if he attempted to escape, or was deemed unworthy to die the honorable death that the seppuku rite provided, a jōiuchi was issued.

⑧ ⑨ ⑩

⑪ ⑫

Customarily, the lord sent a seishi (formal messenger) to the accused in order to notify him of his death sentence. The seishi was accompanied by a sword master as a fukushi (deputy messenger). In the criminal's residence, the seishi took out the official notice, containing the details and nature of the crime, called a jōi (executive order). The fukushi at that point had positioned himself seated behind either the seishi or the accused. As soon as the seishi was about to read out the notification, the fukushi rose, ran toward the accused, and cut him down. The fukushi had to be an educated samurai, and had to follow appropriate samurai manner when he executed the indicted man.

In many cases the accused would have been likely to resist and fight to survive. For this reason, jōiuchi had to be conducted by a budō master proficient not only in kenjutsu and iaijutsu but also in a wide range of martials arts.

When pursuers wearing the official jingasa located the guilty person outdoors, they announced his crime and pronounced the sentence of jōiuchi on the spot.

OKUDEN
(MASTER LEVEL)

Enshin Ryū was founded in the tumultuaous Sengoku period, and as a result it uses jūjutsu based on kumi-uchi hyōhō (a battlefield grappling system). This technique was combined with elements from other martial arts, such as kenjutsu, iaijutsu, bōjutsu, and sōjutsu, among others.

In the okuden level, students study iai techniques that are combined with kenjutsu and jūjutsu, although when seen by the non-initiated, the normal kata has the appearance of iaijutsu. In training in the different elements of the kata, such as battō, tachisabaki, and taisabaki, speed is of the utmost importance. At this level, the student has to develop his fighting skills to the standard of swordsmen who engaged in actual combat.

Tora-no-o ("tiger tail")

This kata teaches how to fight when the swordsman is suddenly forced to confront an enemy who is at an advantage, and has already drawn his sword. The situation is compared to accidentally stepping on the tail of a tiger, hence the kata's name—tora-no-o ("tiger tail").

The iai kata begins with a sudden attack from an enemy who has already drawn his sword, while the swordsman has had no time to draw his. Quickly step in front of the enemy

①

Tora (tiger) is the symbol of fearless attack.

②-A

②-B (supplementaly step)

and execute atemi (in this case to the chest) with the tsuka-gashira (handle-end) of the sword ①–②. Remaining in close proximity to the attacker, unsheathe the sword, and immediately make a tsuki to the attacker's throat ③–⑥.

Urawaza ("hidden techniques") also exist for this kata. These are composed of eighteen variations of tora-no-o, and have been passed down since the Edo period. They are highly developed, secret techniques, also called kumiuchi kenpō, combining swordmanship with jūjutsu.

③

④

⑤

⑥

⑦

⑧

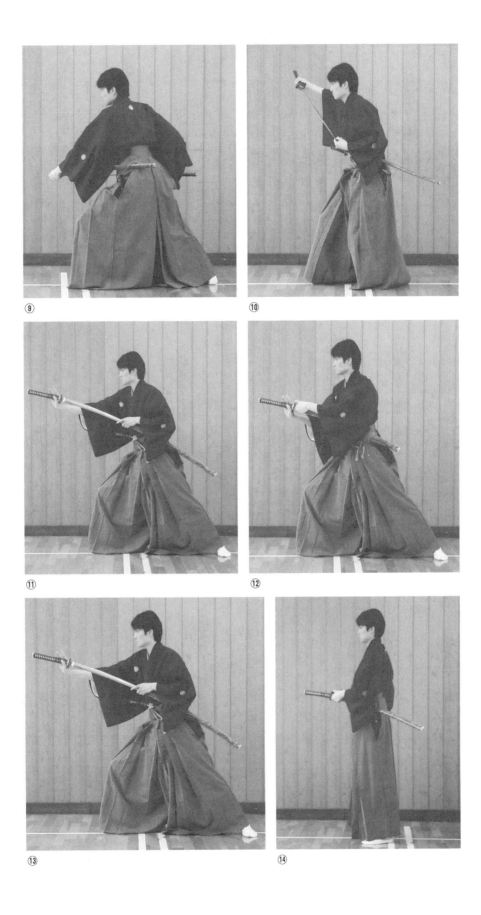

⑨

⑩

⑪

⑫

⑬

⑭

①   ②   ③   ④

⑤   ⑥

⑦   ⑧   ⑨

Shunme ("running horse")

The shunme kata begins with the same situation as that of tora-no-o. When the enemy steps forward to attack, hit the enemy with the tsuka-gashira of the sword ①–②. As the enemy steps back to flee, quickly draw the sword ③, face him in chūdan-no-kamae ④, and, using kobashiri, pursue him, then execute a tsuki ⑤. Assume chūdan-no-kamae again ⑥, and repeat this technique, ⑦–⑩. Assume chūdan-no-kamae ⑪ then conduct kobashiri backward ⑫–⑭, and conduct a further tsuki ⑮. In this kata, the kobashiri, both backward and forward, is of crucial importance, hence the kata's name—shunme, which means "running horse." There is also a more aggressive urawaza in which the swordsman kicks down the enemy.

⑩   ⑪

⑫   ⑬   ⑭

⑮   ⑯   ⑰

⑱   ⑲   ⑳

① ② ③

④ ⑤

Kaiken performed in yoroi (armor).

Kaiken ("opening sword")

After conducting tora-no-o and shunme, perform a migi kesagiri ⑥–⑦.

⑥

⑦

⑧

⑨

⑩

⑪

⑫

⑬

① ② ③

④ ⑤

⑥ ⑦

Heiken ("closing sword")

After conducting tora-no-o and shunme, perform a hidari kesagiri ⑥–⑦.

① ② ③ ④

⑤ ⑥

Ryūken ("dragon sword")

This kata applies the so-called nagatsuki (long thrust). Begin by executing atemi using the tsuka-gashira of the sword ①–③. Unsheathe the sword quickly ④, and conduct nagatsuki ⑤–⑥, in which the sword is extended further than is necessary for a normal tsuki. In this posture, it is as if the swordsman assumes the shape of an attacking dragon; the extended sword becomes the dragon's head and his body the dragon's own.

⑦

⑧

⑨

⑩

⑪

⑫

⑬

⑭

① ② ③

④ ⑤ ⑧

Hiken ("flying sword")

Enshin Ryū teaches that when performing makkō-uchi one should have the feeling of cutting a mountain in the distance with the kissaki (tip) of the sword. Using the sword in this way gives the impression of the sword being thrown clear of the hands. The hiken kata teaches how to cut down an enemy with precisely this sense of throwing the sword toward him. The student also learns a special tenouchi (grip) required to hold the sword in this kind of action. If the student cuts down in the normal way, the curvature of the sword often causes it to be pulled in toward him. In this kata, however, the student learns how to make the cut as straight as possible, to disable an enemy effectively. A feature of this technique is the special long thrust, pictured in ④ and ⑤.

① ② ③ ④

⑤ ⑥ ⑦

Hakuken ("advancing sword")

This kata assumes an opponent attacking from in front. It is necessary to advance abruptly, draw the sword, and cut him straight down with a makkō-giri (frontal cut) ①–⑦. This technique allows no room for hesitation, and must be executed extremely quickly. It should be thought of as a test of courage between the swordsman and his opponent.

① ② ③

④ ⑤

Gusokuken ("talented sword")

This kata assumes an attack occurring from behind while out walking. When the left foot is in front of the right foot, quickly pivot round counterclockwise, simultaneously drawing the sword, and cut the enemy down ①–⑤. The tachisabaki and taisabaki in this kata must be executed harmoniously, just as in the kata of hakuken, and the time between sword-drawing and cutting down in this kata needs to be just as short. Although gusokuken looks simple, it is, in fact, very difficult to master for all those but the most exceptionally talented swordsmen.

The dragon god in the Nō drama *Chikubushima*.

⑥

⑦

⑧

⑨

⑩

⑪

⑫

⑪ ⑫ ⑬

⑭ ⑮ ⑯

Ryūtōken ("flowing sword")

The ryūtōken technique uses the principle of deflection. When crossing swords with an opponent's attack, the technique must, rather than squarely blocking the sword, neutralize the attack by parrying or deflecting it away.

Using the sword to block an opponent's incoming attack is a sign of bad swordsmanship. The sword blade is very sharp and cuts very well but is not really designed to block an attack on the sharp edge of the blade, as this can warp or even break it. And the tsuba (sword guard) serves only to protect the hand against possible injuries, not to block a cut. If an opponent's sword reaches the tsuba of one's own sword, then the results can be fatal.

Thus rather than using a uketome (block) to stop a sword attack, the swordsman should use ukenagashi (deflection). Ukenagashi allows the swordsman to receive an opponent's sword in a flowing way to parry it, and is essential for good swordsmanship.

① ② ③ ④

⑤ ⑥ ⑦

Hidari tenshin ken ("left-whirling sword")

Hidari tenshin ken, as well as the following technique, migi tenshin ken, teaches how to defeat several surrounding enemies. The kata has some resemblance to hakuken and gusokuken. First, cut the enemy with a makkō-giri ①–⑦, and immediately after change position, taking a step to the left while simultaneously bringing the sword horizontally above the head ⑧. Using the right foot as a pivot, turn right 180 degrees, swing the sword vertically upward ⑨, and perform a makkō-giri to an enemy behind ⑩.

① ② ③ ④

⑤ ⑥ ⑦

Migi tenshin ken ("right-whirling sword")

This technique is similar to hidari tenshin ken. First, perform a makkō-giri ①–⑦, then immediately step to the right, bringing the sword horizontally above the head, ⑧. Then, using the left foot as a pivot, turn left 180 degrees, swing the sword vertically upward ⑨–⑩, and again perform a makkō-giri to an enemy behind ⑪.

The makkō-giri and upward swing of the sword can be repeated continuously, and this technique is very useful against multiple opponents coming from as many as eight directions. The combination of footwork and swordwork taught in this technique is therefore of the utmost importance.

CHAPTER 5

KENJUTSU APPLICATIONS

THE SWORD AGAINST OTHER WEAPONS

Swords were the very soul of the warrior, and kenjutsu practitioners developed techniques using swords to defeat an opponent regardless of the weapon he was using. This chapter will introduce some of these techniques.

Sword and Yari

The yari (spear) was one of the most important weapons for warriors on the battlefield. The Sengoku-period warrior used his spear to advance to a higher position. During battle, warriors tried to surpass their rivals by being the first to engage in actual combat and take the head of an important enemy. This was considered a great honor, and those who succeeded were called ichiban-yari ("the person of the first spear").

When fighting an enemy armed with a spear, a short sword is more practical than a long one. The yari is a strong weapon—it can be used very quickly to thrust at an opponent and also has a very long reach. There is a special technique called shibaki yari in which one uses the hosaki (spear head) to beat an opponent's body, and later to cut into them. For a swordsman, it was important to block or parry, upward or downward, the thrusting action, or shibaki, of the yari as fast as possible. For this purpose the short sword was used.

Tenshin Hyōhō's sōjutsu hiten-no-kamae.

Short-sword posture used in Koden Enshin Ryū against a spear.

The yari side assumes hiten-no-kamae ("sky-flying posture"). The swordsman raises his kodachi (short sword) to jōdan-no-kamae.

①

The yari side moves forward and thrusts at the swordsman, who parries this to his left.

②

The yari side retreats and, once again, assumes hiten-no-kamae.

③

The yari side thrusts at the swordsman, who parries this time to his right.

The swordsman quickly moves in and makes a cut to his opponent's wrist.

The yari side assumes tenchi-no-kamae ("posture of heaven and earth"), and prepares to attack.

Just as he is about to thrust, he is stopped by the swordsman, who swiftly parries the spear to his right side.

③

④

⑤

The yari side strikes down at the swordsman from the upper left ③. The swordsman blocks this attack with his short sword ④, and finishes the kata with a cut to his opponent's neck.

Tenshin hyōhō's naginata tenchi-no-kamae ("posture of heaven and earth").

Tenshin Hyōhō's naginata jin-no-kamae ("posture of human being").

Sword and Naginata

The naginata (halberd) was used as a main battlefield weapon throughout the Heian and Kamakura periods (749–1333), but was gradually replaced by the yari (spear). In the Edo period, the naginata was used by the wives and daughters of warriors to defend their house or to fight inside the castle.

The naginata used by women was called ko-naginata (small naginata). Its blade was smaller than that of the naginata used by men on the battlefield. The men's naginata was also called ō-naginata (big naginata).

The naginata was used mainly against the sword. Compared to the sword, however, which is lighter and more easily handled, the naginata, with its especially long hilt and heavy blade, is much slower.

Both sides face each other in seigan-no-kamae (middle posture) ①.

The naginata side raises the naginata and prepares to attack the swordsman's head ②.

The swordsman parries the naginata ③, and deflects it to his right ④.

⑤ The swordsman moves quickly in for the counterattack.

The Nō drama *Funabenkei* (left) and *Kiyotsune*.

① The naginata side assumes uraseigan-no-kamae ("reversed aiming-at-the-eye posture"), the swordsman assumes hassō-no-kamae.

② The naginata side makes an upward cut, which is parried by the swordsman.

③ The naginata side assumes chūdan-jin-no-kamae (middle posture for the naginata).

④ The swordsman parries the naginata and thrusts his sword forward.

① The bō side assumes chūdan-no-kamae. The swordsman assumes hassō-no-kamae.

② The bō side moves forward and thrusts at the swordsman, who blocks with his sword.

Sword and Bō

Bō (stick) fighting arts include techniques from both sōjutsu (spear art) and naginatajutsu (halberd art). The stick has no blade, so there is no distinction between its sides. Because of this, many variations of fighting styles are possible, and bōjutsu (stick fighting art) is a very comprehensive and fast martial art. Another characteristic of the stick is that, because it has no cutting edge, it is possible to defeat an opponent without bloodshed.

③ The swordsman steps forward and traps the bō under his left arm, and at the same time swings his sword.

④ The swordsman counterattacks. (In this technique the swordsman takes advantage of the fact that the staff has no cutting edge.)

① The bō side assumes hidari-no-waki-gamae (left position). The swordsman assumes daijōdan-no-kamae.

The bō side makes an upward
strike to he swordsman, who
parries this with his sword.

②

The bō side takes a step
backward and prepares for
shōmen-uchi (frontal strike).

③

④

The swordsman cuts the bō down
to his right side.

⑤

⑥

The swordsman ends the kata by
attacking his opponent's neck.

⑦

A selection of shuriken.

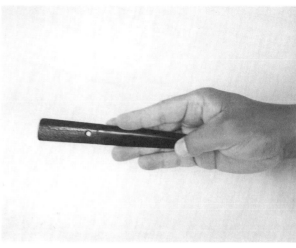

A type of shuriken used for training by the last shogun, Tokugawa Yoshinobu (1837–1913), at the end of the Edo period.

Manji-shuriken

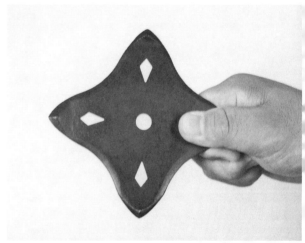

Shihō-ken

Sword and Shuriken

The shuriken, like the bow and arrow, the musket, and the pistol, belongs to the tobi-dōgu (weapons fired at distant enemies). The shuriken was used primarily by the ninja, but all warriors practiced its usage as part of their martial arts training. In order to be able to counter any kind of attack with his sword, a sword master had to be familiar with all weapons.

Jūji-ken

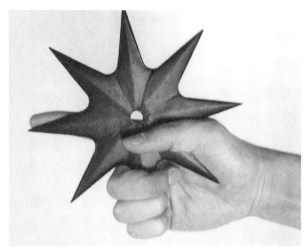

Happō-ken

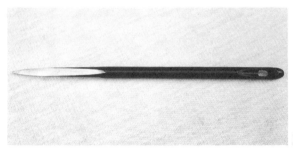

Bōte-shuriken (Ganritsu Ryū shuriken)

The throwing technique of bōte-shuriken.

The target of bōte-shuriken was often the eye of an opponent. The swordsman assumes a posture that allows him to protect his right eye from a shuriken with his sword.

Secret technique using clothing, or any other fabric, as protection against arrows, bullets, or shuriken. This technique was used from the Sengoku period onward.

Defensive posture against a shuriken attack. Note how both body and eyes are protected.

CHAPTER 6

Mutō-dori
Techniques

THE USE OF "NO SWORD"

Warriors originally achieved success by killing their enemies on the battlefield. After the Sengoku period ended, the situation in the country stabilized and during peacetime warriors entered the rank of the nobility. The bushi, who were at the top level of society, wore the sword as a symbol of their authority and power. In a civilized society, gentlemen bushi considered it vulgar and uncivil to draw their sword and kill someone without good reason. It was necessary to develop techniques to defeat an armed opponent without drawing one's own sword or using any other arms. Such techniques are known as mutō-dori, or no-sword techniques. Mutō-dori are considered to be the samurai's ultimate skills in martial arts, and only a true master can accomplish them.

Technique A: Yagyū Shinkage Ryū's Mutō-Dori

Tadashige Watanabe, sōshu of the Yagyū Shinkage Ryū Marobashikai, and his student demonstrating a mutō-dori technique. Yagyū Shinkage Ryū's mutō-dori techniques have been famous since Japan's samurai era. In the technique shown here, the swordsman, starting from daijōdan-no-kamae ①, makes a downward cut to his opponent, who counters this by grabbing the sword's hilt with his left hand ②, while at the same time pushing the swordsman's right elbow with his right hand ③–④. Next, the swordsman is unbalanced and thrown down, after which his sword is taken away ⑤–⑥.

①

②

③

④

⑤

⑥

①

②

Technique B: Koden Enshin Ryū's Shiraha-Dori

Starting from hassō-no-kamae ①, the swordsman tries to make a frontal downward cut. The party performing the mutō-dori stops this by pushing the sword's hilt up with his left hand and taking the sword's miné (back) with his right hand ②. Next, he pushes the blade down with his right hand, and pulls the hilt back with his left hand so the sword is removed from his attacker's hands ③–④. He ends the kata by swinging the sword up and cutting his attacker's jaw ⑤.

③

④

⑤

①

②

Technique C: Kukishin Ryū's Mutō-Dori

The swordsman assumes daijōdan-no-kamae ① and attempts to make a frontal downward cut to his opponent, who stops this by stepping forward and raising his right hand to move inside the attack and avoid being cut by the sword ②. Next, the mutō-dori side puts his right hand on top of the swordsman's right hand ③, immobilizes both the swordsman's arms with his left arm, and kicks him in the groin with his right foot ④.

③

④

①

②

Technique D: Koden Enshin Ryū's Shiraha-Dori

The swordsman thrusts his sword at his opponent ①, who uses his left
hand against the side of the blade and deflects it sideways to the right ②.
Next, the mutō-dori side takes the hilt of the sword with his right hand ③,
and pulls it free from his attacker ④.

③

④

ACKNOWLEDGMENTS

The ethics and merits formulated from the concept of the way of the samurai are still rooted deeply in the psyche of present-day Japanese. Throughout history, with its many wars and battles, many lessons have been drawn. Old principles, such as "When you go to war, you should not lose," or "One should not desire to fight, but instead look for truth and peace," are also borne from these unstable times. In this modest book, I hope to introduce the art and culture of the Japanese warrior, the bushi, the master of war. I will be very happy if the reader, through this work, gains a better understanding of the spirit and culture of the samurai.

For the publication of this book, I am indebted to a great number of people. Particularly to Shirō Ōmiya, author of *The Hidden Roots of Aikido: Aiki Jujutsu Daitōryū*, who introduced me to Kodansha International, and advised me on photo sessions. For an explanation of swordmaking, my thanks goes to Yoshihiro Hamasaki, and Nōshū Iaidō's Keiji Igarashi. For the translation of the Japanese text I owe thanks to Serge Mol, Hisao Kawakami, Norio Yasuda, and Midori Tanaka.

In addition, I would also like to express my gratitude to the following individuals and institutions for their kind cooperation: Chihaya-Akasaka Village Historical Museum Gallery, Eifukuji Temple, Myōkōin Temple, Yanagisawa Library (in Yamato-Kōriyama Castle), Odawara City Museum Library, Shindō Tenshin Ryū sōke Tenshin Kaminaga, Shinkage Ryū sōke Kazutora Toyoshima and shihan Tomoo Koide, Shinkage Ryū Marobashikai sōshu Tadashige Watanabe, Yagyū Shingan Ryū shihan Kaneharu Shimazu, Niten Ichi Ryū shihan Tokisada Imanishi and Akio Yoshimoto, Kanra Kiraku Ryū shike Kohaku Iwai, swordsmiths Kanetoki Kojima and Kanemichi Kojima, kendō shihan Shigenobu Ogino, Kanze Ryū Nōgaku shihan Keiji Hasegawa, Diet member Akira Satō, National Treasure Tajihayahime Shrine, Kodansha International's Tetsuo Kuramochi and the rest of the editorial staff, and all the members of the Nihonkoden-Fūshimusōkai.

BIBLIOGRAPHY

Kojiki ("Record of Ancient Matters," 712)

Nihon shoki ("Chronicle of Japan," 720)

Sonshi-no-Taikeiteki Kenkyū; Kenji Satō, Kazama-shobō (Tokyo, 1963)

Bugeiryūha-daijiten; Kiyoshi Watatani and Tadashi Yamada, Shinjinbutsu-ōraisha (Tokyo, 1969)

Bushido, Inazō Nitobo, translated by Tatsuya Naramoto, Mikasa-shobō (Tokyo, 1993)

Kendō-Hiyō, Miyamoto Musashi, Taiku-to-supōtsu-sha (Tokyo, 2002)

Nipponjin-no-Shiseikan, Yūko Yoshino, Jinbun-shoin (Kyoto, 1995)

Koryū-Kenjutsu, Fumon Tanaka, Airyūdo (Tokyo, 1995)

Koryū-Kenjutsu-Gairon, Fumon Tanaka, Airyūdo (Tokyo, 2000)

Documents from Nihonkoden-Fūshimusōkai's collection

Documents from Fumon Tanaka's collection

PHOTO CREDITS

GLOSSARY

aiuchi   Mutual slaying.

Amaterasu Omi-no-kami   The sun goddess, from the mythological Age of the Gods.

Ashikaga Takauji   Shogun at the end of the Nanbokuchō period (1305-58).

ashisabaki   Footwork.

atemi   Body strike or blow.

aun   Principle of completion and mutual understanding, or of bringing together opposite concepts. It often manifests as a beginning and an ending, or inhalation and exhalation.

bajutsu   Horsemanship.

Batō Kannon   The bodhisattva Kannon with the head of a horse.

battō   Drawing the sword.

bō   Stick.

bōjutsu   Stick fighting art.

budō   Martial arts, or the way of the samurai.

bugaku   Imperial court dance.

bugei jūhappan   The eighteen martial arts.

bujutsu   Martial arts.

bun-bu-ittai   Concept that the martial arts and literature are one and the same.

bun-bu-ryōdō   Concept that the martial arts and literature are separate but equally important.

bushidō   Way of the samurai, or warrior code of honor.

chidō   Law of earth.

chūdachi   Medium-length sword.

chūdan-jin-no-kamae   Middle posture for the naginata.

chūdan-no-kamae   Middle position of the sword.

chūden   Intermediate level.

chūkan kokyū   Special breathing technique: "inhale half, exhale half."

daijōdan-no-kamae   Uppermost attacking position of the sword.

daimyō   Local feudal lord who was a retainer to the shogun.

daitō   Long sword.

dan   Grade.

dō   Way, principal, spiritual path.

dōjō   Practice hall.

Dokkodō   "The Way of Walking Alone": the twenty-one articles of his personal philosophy of life, written by Miyamoto Musashi.

Edo period   Period ruled by the Tokugawa shogunate, 1600-1868.

Ekikyō   "The I-Ching Book of Changes."

en-no-kata   Circular form.

Enshin Ryū   One of the traditional schools of the martial arts.

Fudō Myōō   The god of fire.

fudōshin   Unmovable heart.

fukushi   Deputy messenger.

Futsunomitama-no-tsurugi   According to Japanese mythology, the first sword created, and possessed with divine powers.

Futsunushi-no-mikoto   The guardian deity of the traditional martial arts.

gagaku   Imperial court music.

gedan-no-kamae   Lower position of the sword.

gendai budō   Modern budō.

Genji   A well-known bumon (warrior family).

Genpei no kassen   Heike-Genji conflict, 1180–85.

gishiki   Ritual.

godan   5th dan.

Gōjyū Ryu   A style of karate.

Gorin-no-Sho   "The Book of Five Rings," written by
   Miyamoto Musashi.

gyakute   Reversed gripping.

hakama   Divided skirt.

haku-ryū   White dragon.

hamon   Cutting edge of a sword.

hanbōjutsu   Half-length bōjutsu.

hanshi   Highest rank given to martial arts practitioners.

haori   Coat.

hassō-no-kamae   High position of the sword, the hilt is
   level with the right shoulder.

hachidan   8th dan.

happō   Eight directions.

hara   Stomach, belly; center of gravity.

Heihō Sanjūgokajō   "The Thirty-Five Articles of Strategy," written by Miyamoto Musashi.

Heike   A well-known bumon (warrior family).

henka   Variations.

hidari   Left.

hidari-kesagiri   Left diagonal cut from the opponent's
   neck to the waist.

hidari-kesauchi   Left strike to the opponent's neck.

hidari-waki-no-kamae   Left position of the sword.

hien   Jumping monkey.

hirazukuri-yoroi-dōshi   Armor-piercing dagger with no
   ridgeline.

hitatare   Everyday attire which could also be worn in formal circumstances.

hiten-no-kamae   Sky-flying posture.

hō-no-kata   Square form.

hoko   Early type of spear.

hosaki   Spear head.

hyōhō   Battlefield grappling system; also refers to general
   strategy.

iai   Fast sword-technique.

iaijutsu   Fast sword-fighting.

ichiban-yari   The person of the first spear.

igeta   Form of parallel crosses.

inazuma   Sudden flash of lightning.

ittō   One sword.

jige   Peasant.

jin-no-kamae   Posture of human being.

jindō   Law of mankind.

Jinmu Tennō   First emperor of Japan.

jindachi   Sword designed specifically for use on the battlefield.

jitte   Hand-held weapon similar to a dagger, with a long
   guard.

jitte dori technique   Capturing and binding an opponent
   using a jitte.

jo-ha-kyū   Principle of a beginning, a middle, and an end.

jōdan-no-kamae   Upper position of the sword.

jōi   Executive order.

jōiuchi   Execution order from a feudal lord; to kill on
   higher orders.

Jōkyū-no-ran   Jōkyū Disturbance, 1221.

judō   Sport based on classical jūjutsu, developed by Kanō
   Jigorō.

jūjutsu   Fighting art in which one stops an opponent's
   attack without using weapons; the original meaning is
   "the gentle art."

jūkendō   Method using budō principles to develop the
   mind and body of the practitioners. Its techniques are
   based on Japanese classical spear fighting.

jutsu   Art, technique.

juttejutsu   Capturing and tying up an opponent.

jūdan   10th dan.

kabuki   Classical Japanese theater.

kabuto   Helmet.

kaiden   Deep initiation.

kaishaku   Performing a decapitation to assist a warrior committing seppuku.

kamae   Stance, posture.

Kamakura period   Historical period that saw the first military government ruled by shoguns, 1192-1333.

kamishimo   Formal wear.

kamon   Family crest.

karate   Traditional martial art from Okinawa.

kariginu   Clothing worn by warriors for formal ceremonies.

kata   Form.

kata guruma   A throwing technique.

katana   Style of sword originally called katakiriba; it had a straight body and a single cutting edge.

keikogi   Practice uniform.

ken   Seeing.

Kendō   Literally, "the way of the sword," a sport which uses protective clothing and bamboo safety swords.

kenjutsu   Sword art, also called kenpō.

kensei-no-kamae   Posture in which the sword is extended forward to prevent enemies from advancing.

kiriai   Two swordsmen each attacking, with two cuts each at their opponent.

kissaki   Tip of the sword.

kobashiri   A way of running using very small steps.

kodachi   Short sword.

ko-naginata   Small naginata.

kōbō ittai   Principle in which attack and defense are executed simultaneously.

kobudō   Classical budō; traditional martial arts.

kodachi   Short sword.

Koden Enshin Ryū   A style of kobudo.

kogarasumaru   Sword with a curvature and two cutting edges extending about half the length of the blade.

Kojiki   "Record of Ancient Matters," 712.

kosode   Small-sleeved kimono.

kumiuchi   Jūjutsu.

Kusunoki Masashige   A warrior-general, a hero in the Nanbokuchō period (?–1336).

kuttō   Sword with a single cutting edge on the inside of the curvature.

kyōshi   Second-highest rank given to martial arts practitioners.

kyūdan   9th dan.

kyūjutsu   Archery.

kyūsho   Vulnerable parts of the body.

makimono   Scroll.

makkō-giri   Frontal cut.

makkō-uchi   Frontal strike.

Mari Shiten   The god of self-defense and victory.

Masamune   Swordsmith widely recognized as the founder of modern sword-forging techniques.

men   Front of the head.

menkyo   Licences.

metezashi   Short sword hung on the right side.

metsubushi   Attack to the eyes.

migi   Right.

migi-kesagiri   Right diagonal cut from the opponent's neck to the waist.

migi-kesauchi   Right strike to the opponent's neck.

migi-waki-no-kamae   Right position of the sword.

Mikkyō   Esoteric Buddhism.

Minamoto no Yoritomo   Founder of the Kamakura Shogunate (1147–99).

miné   Blunt edge of the sword.

Miyamoto Musashi   Famous samurai and swordman (1584?–1645).

mononofu   Ancient samurai, the earliest warriors.

mu   The void, nothingness.

musōken   "No-thought sword."

mutō dori   "No-sword technique," the samurai's ultimate skill in martial arts.

nagamaki   Weapon with a long blade, combining sword and naginata.

nagatsuki   Long thrust.

naginata   Halberd.

naginatajutsu   Halberd fighting art.

nanadan   7th dan.

Nanbokuchō period   The Northern and Southern Courts period, 1337–92.

nidan   2nd dan.

Nihon Shoki   "Chronicle of Japan," 720.

nihontō   Japanese sword.

ninja   Mercenary agent highly trained in martial arts.

ninjutsu   Ninja technique.

Niten Ichi Ryū   Sword style created by Miyamoto Musashi.

nitō   Two swords.

nitō-ken   Two-sword techniques.

nitō-yaburi   Techniques developed to counterattack and overcome nitō using only one sword.

Nitta Yoshisada   A famous warrior-general (1301–38).

Nōgaku (Nō drama)   One of Japan's oldest traditional performing arts, initially called *sarugaku*.

nodachi   Very long sword; also known as ōdachi. Its original meaning is field sword.

nōtō   Sheathing the sword.

nukitsuke   Fast drawing and cutting.

ō-naginata   Big naginata.

obi   Belt.

ōchō bunka   Court culture.

ōdachi   Long sword; also known as nodachi.

okuden   Master level.

Ōnin-no-ran   Ōnin War, 1467–77.

reigi   Courtesy, etiquette, protocol.

renshi   A high rank given to martial arts practitioners.

rokkan   The sixth sense.

rokudan   6th dan.

ryūgi   Style.

ryūha   School.

Ryūkyū   Historical kingdom; it became the prefecture of Okinawa in the Meiji period.

ryūso   Founder of a school.

sakki   Intention to kill.

samurai   Warrior; deriving from "saburomono," meaning "he who awaits orders."

sandan   3rd dan.

saya   Scabbard.

seigan-no-kamae   "Aiming-at-the-eye posture," middle posture.

seishi   Formal messenger.

seiza   Formal sitting position; formal kneeling posture.

Sengoku period   Warring States period, 1467–1568.

seppuku   The ritual taking of one's life; hara-kiri.

seppuku-tō   Sword used by the samurai conducting seppuku.

shidachi   Party who defends and counterattacks during technique training.

shihan   Students of the sōke who have become masters and taken on students themselves.

shihō   Four directions.

shimei gamae   Fatal-blow position. Also known as todome gamae.

shinai   Bamboo safety sword.

shini-shōzoku   Costume worn in preparation for death.

Shinto   Early folklore and religion in Japan.

shirasaya   Plain scabbard.

Shitō Ryū   A style of karate.

shodan   1st dan.

shoden   Beginning level.

shogun   Military dictator, the head of the samurai.

shogun gaku   Study to become shogun.

Shōmen-uchi   Frontal strike.

Shōrinji kenpō   A style of karate in China.

shōtō   Short sword.

Shōtōkan Ryū   A style of karate.

Shōtoku-taishi   Prince regent to empress Suiko (r. 593–628).

shurikenjutsu   Knife throwing.

sōjutsu   Spear art.

sōke   Head of a school, sometimes also called sōshu.

sonkyo   Squatting position.

sōshu   Head of a school, also referred to as sōke.

sōujtsu   Spear fighting

suemonogiri   Cutting test performed on objects (such as bamboo and straw) that are not secured to the ground. The test was an indication of the samurai's skills.

suishin gamae   Downward position, as if holding a fishing line straight into a pool.

suki   Unguarded moments.

sundome   Very difficult technique —after performing a cut or a thrust, the practitioner must ensure that the blade stops just before touching the opponent's body.

tachi   Sword.

tachisabaki   Sword manipulation.

taitō   Possession of the sword in the obi.

Takeda Shingen (1521–73)   A great warlord of the Sengoku period.

Takemikazuchi-no-mikoto   The guardian deity of the traditional martial arts.

tameshigiri   Cutting test that served to demonstrate the sharpness and quality of a sword.

tatami   Mat.

teiōgaku   Study of the emperor.

tenchi-no-kamae   Posture of heaven and earth.

tendō   Law of the universe.

tengu   Mythical creatures with long beaks and wings living deep in the mountains.

tenouchi   Grip.

tobi-dōgu   Projectiles; weapons fired at distant enemies.

Tokugawa Ieyasu   Warrior chieftain who founded the Tokugawa Shogunate (1543–1616).

tora-no-o   Tiger tail.

tori   Person who responds to an attack; defender.

torii   The gate of a Shinto shrine.

torii-gamae   Upper guard position; the shape resembles the gate of a Shinto shrine.

torinawajutsu   Capturing and binding using a rope.

Toyotomi Hideyoshi   Warlord who finally managed to unify the nation (1537–98).

tsuba   Sword guard.

Tsuchigumo   Earth Spider, a mythical monster.

tsuka   Hilt.

tsuka-gashira   Handle-end, top of the hilt.

tsuki   Thrust.

tsurugi   Sword with double cutting edge, referred to from mythological times.

uchidachi   Attacker.

Uesugi Kenshin (1530–78)   A great warlord of the Sengoku period.

uke   Person who initiates an attack, attacker.

ukemi   Breakfall.

ukenagashi   Deflection.

uketome   Block.

uraseigan-no-kamae   Reversed aiming-at-the-eye posture.

urawaza   Hidden technique.

waki-gamae   Guard position with the sword to one's side to conceal the arm.

wakizashi   Sub-sword, side sword, or short sword, which hung on the left side.

waza   Technique.

Yagyū Hyōgonosuke   The third generation of the Yagyū Shinkage Ryū (1579–1650).

Yagyū Shingan Ryū   Famous style and sect of the traditional Japanese sword.

Yamato   Former capital, the present-day city of Tenri, in Nara prefecture.

yari   Spear.

yodan   4th dan.

yoroi   Armor.

yoroi-dōshi   Sword used for thrusting into an enemy's body through gaps in the armor (yoroi); an armor-piercing dagger without a ridgeline.

yumitori   Archer.

zanshin-no-kamae   State of mental awareness of the opponent and surroundings after completion of a technique.

INDEX

Fumon Tanaka was born in 1943. He started learning kendō at the age of thirteen, and has been practicing martial arts ever since. He is the leading authority on the traditional martial arts in Japan, and has published many books on the subject. In 1988 he traveled to France as part of the Nihon Budō delegation selected by the Ministry of Education and the Agency for Cultural Affairs. Since then he has frequently been invited to teach in Germany, Italy, England, France, Denmark, and Sweden.

TITLES AND LICENSES HELD BY THE AUTHOR

Modern kendō, fourth dan

Modern bōjutsu, fifth dan

Jūjutsu (kumiuchi hyōhō yawara-no-jutsu), seventh dan

Kyōshi battōjutsu, seventh dan

Kyōshi iai suemonogiri kenpō, seventh dan

Hanshi kobudō, eighth dan

Traditional budō Hanshi titles and licenses held by the author:

1. Koden Enshin Ryū kumiuchi kenden 11th sōke

2. Kukishin Ryū bujutsu 19th sōke

3. Honmon Enshin Ryū iai suemonogiri kenpō 4th sōke

4. Tenshin Hyōhō Sōden Kukamishin Ryū 19th sōke

5. Kotō Ryū representative sōke

6. Shindō Tenshin Ryū toritejutsu representative sōke

7. Hontai Takagi Yōshin Ryū jūjutsu representative sōke

8. Asayamaichiden Ryū taijutsu representative sōke

9. Shinden Fudō Ryū representative sōke

10. Bokuden Ryū jūjutsu koshinomawari representative sōke

11. Kōga Ryū ninjutsu

12. Iga Ryū ninpō

13. A one-time director of Dainihon-Butokukai

14. A standing adviser of Zennihon-Budō-Sōgōrenmei

President of Nihonkoden-Fūshimusōkai